HAMLYN

London · New York
Sydney · Toronto

Hamlyn All Colour Freezer Cook Book

Audrey Ellis

full colour
freezing recipes
with illustrated
freezing hints

Published by
The Hamlyn Publishing Group Limited
London . New York . Sydney . Toronto
Astronaut House, Feltham, Middlesex, England

Photography by John Lee
Line drawings by Ann Rees

ISBN 0 600 33614 X

Printed in Hong Kong

Contents

Introduction

Readers acclaim the Hamlyn All Colour Cook Book because it gives them exactly the help and encouragement they need to try out new recipes. On page after page of this big, beautiful cook book, a full colour illustration of each dish is to be found, immediately above the recipe. The instructions are clearly and simply set out; and below each recipe comes a useful quick cooking tip. Enthusiastic cooks, both experts and beginners, tell me a colour photograph of the finished dish inspires confidence to try out an unfamiliar recipe. The Hamlyn All Colour Cook Book has brought readers exactly this inspiration; and now to join it comes a companion volume, the Hamlyn All Colour Freezer Cook Book. I thoroughly enjoyed creating and testing these new recipes to make better use of my own freezer, and you may be sure I have planned each section and chosen each recipe to bring the greatest enjoyment and benefit to my readers.

Now that economy is the new watchword, the real advantages of cooking for your freezer become apparent. You will want to try soups, which cost little in money and effort, yet can taste utterly delicious; and other meal starters that are often expensive to buy, like Anchovied terrine of pork, which look and taste even better when home-made. Then come the easy economy recipes and cheerful casseroles; these make good use of pasta and rice (now serious competitors to the much-loved potato), all kinds of sausages, and the less expensive meats for slow-cooking flavourful casseroles, like Kidneys in redcurrant sauce, which the family will love. Poultry dishes, which follow, while often appetising enough for party menus, are still tremendously good value. Baking your own bread is a rewarding experience, and the bread has the special flavour that only home cooking can give. Cautious cooks might begin by using a packaged bread mix, which is simplicity itself to handle. Pastries and puddings, together with cakes and cookies, have always been the pride of an expert home cook. It is the original touch that is needed, as I hope you will agree when you try Coconut apple wedge and Gingered chocolate cheesecake.

For those who must pass these goods by in the freezer centre, on the grounds of cost, there is new inspiration for the most gorgeous frozen desserts including unusual ice creams and impressive gâteaux. How does Iced mocha meringue appeal? It's one of my favourites. The party menus at the end of the book sound elaborate but are as easy to create as all the other dishes; and essential extras, including basic sauces, have not been forgotten.

Fina'ly, I must mention the microwave oven, and the new possibilities this offers to all freezer owners: the ability to transfer dishes straight from the freezer to the oven, without defrosting, and have a piping hot meal on the table in a matter of minutes.

I have experienced so much pleasure in writing this book and seeing how exciting the dishes appear in the delightful colour photographs, that I have every confidence you too will enjoy these new adventures in cooking for your freezer.

Useful facts and figures

Notes on metrication

In this book quantities are given in metric and Imperial measures. Exact conversion from Imperial to metric measures does not usually give very convenient working quantities and so the metric measures have been rounded off into units of 25 grams. The table below shows the recommended equivalents.

Ounces	Approx. g to nearest whole figure	Recommended conversion to nearest unit of 25
1	28	25
2	57	50
3	85	75
4	113	100
5	142	150
6	170	175
7	198	200
8	227	225
9	255	250
10	283	275
11	312	300
12	340	350
13	368	375
14	397	400
15	425	425
16 (1 lb)	454	450
17	482	475
18	510	500
19	539	550
20	567	575

Note: When converting quantities over 20 oz first add the appropriate figures in the centre column, then adjust to the nearest unit of 25. As a general guide, 1 kg (1000 g) equals 2.2 lb or about 2 lb 3 oz. This method of conversion gives good results in nearly all cases, although in certain pastry and cake recipes a more accurate conversion is necessary to produce a balanced recipe.

Liquid measures The millilitre has been used in this book and the following table gives a few examples.

Imperial	Approx ml to nearest whole figure	Recommended ml
¼ pint	142	150 ml
½ pint	283	300 ml
¾ pint	425	450 ml
1 pint	567	600 ml
1½ pints	851	900 ml
1¾ pints	992	1000 ml (1 litre)

Spoon measures All spoon measures given in this book are level unless otherwise stated.

Can sizes At present, cans are marked with the exact (usually to the nearest whole number) metric equivalent of the Imperial weight of the contents, so we have followed this practice when giving can sizes.

Herbs The herbs used in the recipes are fresh unless stated otherwise.

Flour Unless specified, either plain or self-raising flour can be used in the recipes.

Pastry The weights given in the recipes using home-made shortcrust pastry are based on that amount of flour used, while for shop bought frozen puff pastry it is the total weight.

Oven temperatures
The table below gives recommended equivalents.

	°F	°C	Gas Mark
Very cool	225	110	$\frac{1}{4}$
	250	120	$\frac{1}{2}$
Cool	275	140	1
	300	150	2
Moderate	325	160	3
	350	180	4
Moderately hot	375	190	5
	400	200	6
Hot	425	220	7
	450	230	8
Very hot	475	240	9

Note: When making any of the recipes in this book, only follow one set of measures as they are not interchangeable.

Notes for American and Australian users
In America the 8-oz measuring cup is used. In Australia metric measures are now used in conjunction with the standard 250-ml measuring cup. The Imperial pint, used in Britain and Australia, is 20 fl oz, while the American pint is 16 fl oz. It is important to remember that the Australian tablespoon differs from both the British and American tablespoons; the table below gives a comparison. The British standard tablespoon, which has been used throughout this book, holds 17.7 ml, the American 14.2 ml, and the Australian 20 ml. A teaspoon holds approximately 5 ml in all three countries.

British	American	Australian
1 teaspoon	1 teaspoon	1 teaspoon
1 tablespoon	1 tablespoon	1 tablespoon
2 tablespoons	3 tablespoons	2 tablespoons
$3\frac{1}{2}$ tablespoons	4 tablespoons	3 tablespoons
4 tablespoons	5 tablespoons	$3\frac{1}{2}$ tablespoons

An Imperial/American guide to solid and liquid measures

Solid measures

IMPERIAL	AMERICAN
1 lb butter or margarine	2 cups
1 lb flour	4 cups
1 lb granulated or castor sugar	2 cups
1 lb icing sugar	3 cups
1 lb minced meat	2 cups
2 oz fresh breadcrumbs	1 cup
4 oz chopped nuts	1 cup
5 oz dried fruit	1 cup
8 oz rice	1 cup

Liquid measures

IMPERIAL	AMERICAN
$\frac{1}{4}$ pint liquid	$\frac{2}{3}$ cup liquid
$\frac{1}{2}$ pint	$1\frac{1}{4}$ cups
$\frac{3}{4}$ pint	2 cups
1 pint	$2\frac{1}{2}$ cups
$1\frac{1}{2}$ pints	$3\frac{3}{4}$ cups
2 pints	5 cups ($2\frac{1}{2}$ pints)

The list below gives some American equivalents or substitutes for terms and commodities used in this book.

Equipment and terms

BRITISH/AMERICAN	
flan tin/pie pan	liquidise(r)/blend(er)
frying pan/skillet	mould/mold
greaseproof paper/waxed paper	piping bag/pastry bag
grill/broil	sandwich tin/layer cake pan
kitchen paper/paper towels	star nozzle/fluted nozzle
	stoned/pitted

Ingredients

BRITISH/AMERICAN	
aubergine/eggplant	mixed peel/candied peel
beetroot/beet	orange jelly/orange-flavored gelatin
biscuit/cookie or cracker	
black treacle/molasses	peeled prawn/shelled shrimp
cake mixture/cake batter	
castor or granulated sugar/sugar	pig's liver/pork liver
cocoa powder/unsweetened cocoa	plain chocolate/semi-sweet chocolate
cooking apple/baking apple	plain flour/all-purpose flour
cornflour/cornstarch	puff pastry/puff paste
crystallised ginger/candied ginger	scone/biscuit
demerara sugar/brown sugar	self-raising flour/self-rising flour or all-purpose flour sifted with baking powder
double cream/heavy cream	
essence/extract	
gelatine/gelatin	shortcrust pastry/basic pie dough
gherkin/sweet dill pickle	
glacé cherry/candied cherry	single cream/light cream
golden syrup/maple syrup	spring onion/scallion
ham/cured or smoked ham	stem ginger/preserved ginger
icing/frosting	
icing sugar/confectioners' sugar	streaky bacon rasher/bacon slice
lard/shortening	sultana/seedless white raisin
minced beef/ground beef	tomato purée/tomato paste

Soups and starters

Make these unusual soups when the fresh vegetables and other ingredients are at the peak of their season and lowest in price, to enjoy all round the year. The recipes are intended to produce a relatively small quantity of concentrated soup which, according to taste, you can extend by adding a little extra milk or water at serving time. Once you are certain you enjoy the flavour it will be easy to multiply the quantities and make up these soups in bulk.

Or try your hand at some of the deliciously different starters and appetisers here — worthy of the grandest meal.

1 Brussels sprout soup

(illustrated on back of jacket)

You will need . . .

Cooking time
about 30 minutes

Storage time
4–6 months

Defrosting time
6 hours at room temperature

675 g/1½ lb Brussels sprouts, trimmed
50 g/2 oz butter
1 tablespoon flour
1 litre/1¾ pints chicken stock
salt and pepper
4 tablespoons double cream
When serving:
4 tablespoons double cream

Cook the prepared sprouts in boiling salted water until tender. Drain well.

Melt the butter in a large saucepan, add the sprouts, sprinkle over the flour and stir well. Gradually add the stock and bring to the boil, stirring all the time. Cook, uncovered, until the sprouts are very soft.

Blend the soup in a liquidiser or press through a sieve. Add salt and pepper to taste. Stir in the cream until completely smooth and blended. Cool.

To freeze: Pack in a polythene container or foil or poly-thene-lined carton. Seal and label.
To serve: Defrost while still sealed in the pack then reheat gently in a saucepan to boiling point. Swirl 1 tablespoon of cream into each portion of soup.
Serves 4

2 Cream of cucumber soup

You will need . . .

Cooking time
25 minutes

Storage time
4–6 months

Defrosting
Reheat from frozen in a saucepan

1 large cucumber
1 medium onion
2 chicken stock cubes
900 ml/1½ pints boiling water
25 g/1 oz butter
25 g/1 oz flour
When serving:
150 ml/¼ pint milk
2 egg yolks
4 tablespoons cream
chopped mint

Peel the cucumber, halve and quarter the halves length-wise. Discard any noticeable seeds. Chop the onion finely. Make up the stock cubes with the boiling water and use to simmer the onion and cucumber pieces until the vegetables are tender. Sieve or blend in a liquidiser.

Rinse out the pan, melt the butter in it, stir in the flour and cook for 2 minutes, stirring all the time. Add the vegetable purée and stir over gentle heat until the mixture becomes smooth and slightly thickened. Do not allow to boil. Cool.

To freeze: Pack in a polythene container or foil or polythene-lined carton. Seal and label.
To serve: Turn the frozen soup into a saucepan, add the milk and bring slowly to the boil, stirring frequently. Remove from the heat. Beat together the egg yolks and cream and add to the soup, stirring briskly. Reheat but do not allow to boil. Garnish the soup with chopped mint.
Serves 4

FREEZING HINT

Damaged or partially spoiled fruit and vegetables are often on offer at give-away prices just before shops and stalls close for the weekend. Extra supplies can be put to good use for such items as soups or purées for freezing.

FREEZING HINT

Although cucumber is not suitable for eating raw after it has been frozen, it can be grated for use in soups and sauces, or diced and lightly sautéed in butter and then frozen to serve as a cooked vegetable.

Danish
3 cauliflower cheese soup

Leek
4 and artichoke cream

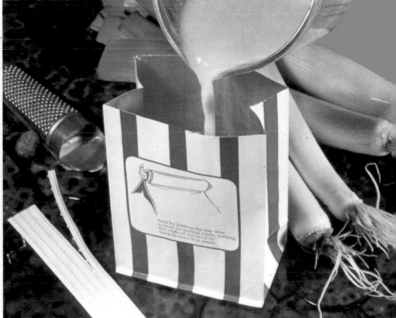

You will need . . .	1 large cauliflower 2 medium onions, chopped
Cooking time 15 minutes	1 litre/1¾ pints water 2 chicken stock cubes 150 ml/¼ pint milk
Storage time 4–6 months	salt and pepper *When serving:* 50 g/2 oz blue cheese, coarsely grated
Defrosting Reheat from frozen in a saucepan	

You will need . . .	450 g/1 lb Jerusalem artichokes 450 g/1 lb leeks 50 g/2 oz butter
Cooking time 25–30 minutes	2 chicken stock cubes 900 ml/1½ pints boiling water ½ teaspoon ground nutmeg
Storage time 4–6 months	salt and pepper *When serving:* 150 ml/¼ pint milk
Defrosting Reheat from frozen in a saucepan	4 tablespoons double cream

Divide the cauliflower into florets and place these in a saucepan with the onion, water and crumbled stock cubes. Bring to the boil, cover and simmer gently for 10–15 minutes, until the vegetables are tender. Liquidise or sieve the mixture.

Rinse the saucepan and return the soup. Stir in the milk and reheat. Adjust the seasoning and cool.

To freeze: Pack in a polythene container. Seal and label.
To serve: Turn the frozen soup into a saucepan and reheat very slowly to boiling point, stirring frequently. Remove from the heat and stir most of the grated cheese into the soup. Garnish with the remaining cheese.
Serves 4

Carefully peel the artichokes. Thickly slice the leeks, discarding all the dark green parts. Wash thoroughly in a colander.

Melt the butter in a heavy saucepan and add the leek. Cover and cook gently for 3 minutes, or until limp. Add the artichokes and cook, covered, for a further 3 minutes. Stir well and pour on the stock cubes made up with the boiling water, and the nutmeg. Cover the pan again and simmer gently until the vegetables are tender. Taste and adjust the seasoning.

Sieve or blend in a liquidiser and cool.

To freeze: Pack in a polythene container or foil or polythene-lined carton. Seal and label.
To serve: Turn the frozen soup into a saucepan, add the milk and reheat very gently to boiling point. Swirl a tablespoon of cream into each plate of soup.
Serves 4

FREEZING HINT

The bland flavour of cauliflower makes it a perfect partner for all sorts of cheeses. Instead of blue cheese, try Cheddar, Gouda, Emmenthal or Gruyère, all of which would be delicious.

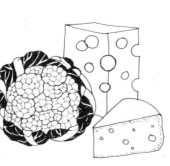

FREEZING HINT

This soup is equally good served cold. Whisk the milk into the defrosted soup, chill and serve swirled with cream as above.

5 Sparkling beetroot soup

6 Green summer soup

5 Sparkling beetroot soup

You will need . . .

Cooking time
40 minutes

Storage time
4–6 months

Defrosting
Reheat from frozen in a saucepan

1 large raw beetroot (about 225 g/8 oz)
100 g/4 oz carrot, grated
100 g/4 oz onion, grated
2 chicken stock cubes
generous 1 litre/2 pints
  boiling water
salt and pepper
When serving:
fried bread croûtons (see recipe 16)

Peel the beetroot. Cut one quarter of it into neat small dice and grate the remainder.

Place the grated beetroot in a saucepan with the other vegetables and pour over the stock cubes made up with the boiling water. Bring to the boil, stirring well. Cover the pan and simmer for about 30 minutes, until all the vegetables are soft.

Strain the liquid off into a clean saucepan and add seasoning to taste. Add the diced beetroot, bring to the boil and cook for 7 minutes. Cool.

To freeze: Pack in a polythene container or foil or polythene-lined carton. Seal and label.
To serve: Turn the frozen soup into a saucepan and reheat gently to boiling point, stirring frequently. Serve with croûtons.
Serves 4

6 Green summer soup

You will need . . .

Cooking time
40–45 minutes

Storage time
4–6 months

Defrosting
Reheat from frozen in a saucepan

1 large lettuce
4 large leaves spinach
6 spring onions, trimmed
25 g/1 oz butter
2 tablespoons flour
600 ml/1 pint milk
½ teaspoon dried thyme
long strip lemon rind
salt and pepper

Wash the lettuce and spinach leaves carefully and shred them. Chop the spring onions.

Melt the butter, add the lettuce, spinach and spring onion and cook gently for 5 minutes. Stir in the flour and cook for a further 3 minutes. Gradually add the milk, thyme, lemon rind, seasoning to taste and bring to the boil, stirring all the time. Cover and simmer for 30 minutes.

Remove the lemon rind. Blend the soup in a liquidiser or press through a sieve. Cool.

To freeze: Pack in a polythene container or foil or polythene-lined carton. Seal and label.
To serve: Turn the frozen soup into a saucepan and reheat very slowly to boiling point, stirring frequently. Taste and adjust the seasoning.
Serves 4

FREEZING HINT

Fried bread croûtons make use of stale bread and keep well in the freezer for short periods. Allow them to cool completely before packing, and reheat on a baking tray in the oven.

FREEZING HINT

To thicken a thin soup when reheating after freezing, add a few small cubes of frozen beurre manié (equal quantities of butter and flour well blended) to the saucepan. Stir constantly until completely dissolved. Let the soup come to the boil and cook for 1 minute.

7 Polish plum soup

You will need . . .

Cooking time
20 minutes

Storage time
4–6 months

Defrosting time
8 hours in the refrigerator

1 kg/2 lb red plums
150 ml/¼ pint orange juice
225 g/ 8 oz raisins
900 ml/1½ pints water
100 g/4 oz sugar
12 cloves
8 g/¼ oz gelatine
150 ml/¼ pint white vermouth
When serving:
150 ml/¼ pint soured cream
little grated orange zest

Stone the plums and place in a saucepan with the orange juice, raisins, water, sugar and cloves.

Bring to the boil and cook, uncovered, for 15 minutes.

Strain the liquid, pressing as much liquid as possible from the fruit, and sprinkle in the gelatine. Stir until it is completely dissolved. Add the vermouth and cool.

To freeze: Pack in a polythene container or foil or polythene-lined carton. Seal and label.
To serve: Defrost while still sealed in the pack. Stir well and serve chilled. Garnish each plate of soup with a spoonful of cream and a sprinkling of grated orange zest.
Serves 4

8 Peppered avocado soup

You will need . . .

Storage time
4–6 months

Defrosting
Reheat from frozen in a saucepan

1 large tomato
1 large ripe avocado
1 tablespoon grated onion
300 ml/½ pint chicken stock
2 tablespoons lemon juice
¼ teaspoon salt
¼ teaspoon chilli sauce or Tabasco sauce
When serving:
300 ml/½ pint milk

Pour boiling water over the tomato, allow to stand for 1 minute then drain and skin. Remove the seeds and cut the flesh into small dice. Cut the avocado in half, peel and remove the stone.

Blend the avocado flesh in a liquidiser with the onion, chicken stock, lemon juice and seasonings. Stir in the diced tomato.

To freeze: Pack in a polythene container or foil or polythene-lined carton. Seal and label.
To serve: Turn the frozen soup into a saucepan and add the milk. Reheat gently to boiling point, stirring frequently, but do not allow to boil.
Serves 3–4

FREEZING HINT

This spiced soup is ideal to serve as a light dessert after a hearty main course. Decorate with a swirl of fresh double cream instead of soured cream.

FREEZING HINT

The ingredients for this soup make a good party dip if the chicken stock and milk are omitted and replaced by 75 g/3 oz cream cheese. Beat well until the mixture is smooth and serve with small cocktail biscuits.

9 Tomato sardine starter

Anchovied 10 terrine of pork

You will need . . .

1 (100-g/4-oz) can sardines in tomato sauce
75 g/3 oz butter
50 g/2 oz soft brown breadcrumbs
grated zest and juice of ½ lemon
2 teaspoons chopped parsley
salt and pepper
When serving:
lemon twists
sprigs of parsley

Storage time
3–4 months

Defrosting time
4 hours at room temperature or
8 hours in the refrigerator

Remove backbones and tails from sardines and mash them with the tomato sauce. Melt the butter, stir in the breadcrumbs and allow to stand for 5 minutes.

Beat in the mashed sardines, lemon zest and juice, parsley and seasoning to taste.

Divide among 4 ramekin dishes or individual containers.

To freeze: Cover the ramekins closely with foil. Seal and label.
To serve: Defrost, garnish with lemon twists and parsley sprigs and serve with hot brown rolls (see recipe 160).
Serves 4

You will need . . .

350 g/12 oz pig's liver
350 g/12 oz belly of pork
8 anchovy fillets
25 g/1 oz butter
1 teaspoon anchovy oil
50 g/2 oz onion, finely chopped
salt and pepper
1 teaspoon ground nutmeg
2 tablespoons flour
150 ml/¼ pint dry white wine
2 eggs
6 rashers streaky bacon

Cooking time
1½ hours

Oven setting
180°C, 350°F, Gas Mark 4

Storage time
4–6 months

Defrosting time
6 hours at room temperature or
8 hours in the refrigerator

Mince the liver, pork and anchovies finely. Melt the butter with the oil, and cook the onion until pale golden. Mix in the minced meat and anchovies, seasoning and nutmeg.

Blend the flour with a little wine to form a thin paste, then combine with the lightly beaten eggs and remaining wine. Pour into the meat mixture and blend well together with a fork or by hand. Remove rind from the bacon. Use rashers to line the base of two 20 × 10-cm/8 × 4-inch foil dishes. Pack in the mixture.

Place in a bain-marie and cook in a moderate oven for 1½ hours. Remove and cool.

To freeze: Slice the pâté and interleave with greaseproof paper or leave in foil container whole. Cover closely with foil. Seal and label.
To serve: Defrost and serve with Melba toast.
Serves 8–10

FREEZING HINT

If you use kitchen foil, which is not heavy gauge, overwrap in clean used foil. This will not come into contact with the food but will give extra protection.

FREEZING HINT

Freeze pâté cut into slices and wrapped individually for quick defrosting. Ideal for picnics or packed lunches.

11 Creamy chicken liver pâté

You will need . . .

Cooking time
45 minutes

Storage time
4–6 months

Defrosting time
3–4 hours at room temperature or
8 hours in the refrigerator

450 g/1 lb pie veal
75 g/3 oz butter
150 ml/¼ pint strong chicken stock
450 g/1 lb chicken livers, trimmed
1 large onion
1 clove garlic
salt and pepper
2 tablespoons dry sherry
bay leaves
lemon slices, quartered

Put the veal with half the butter and the stock into a heavy saucepan and simmer covered, for 30 minutes. Add the chicken livers and continue to cook covered for a further 15 minutes. Meanwhile chop the onion finely, crush the garlic, and cook gently in the remaining butter until pale golden. Add the seasoning and sherry. Combine the veal mixture with the onion mixture and put in a liquidiser. Blend for 30 seconds, or longer if you like a very smooth texture. Taste and adjust for seasoning if necessary.

Spoon into small ramekin dishes. Place a bay leaf and quartered lemon slices on top of each and cool.

To freeze: Cover the ramekins closely with foil, seal and label.
To serve: Defrost and serve with freshly made toast.
Serves 6–8

12 Highlander's game pâté

You will need . . .

Cooking time
About 1 hour 10 minutes

Oven setting
180°C, 350°F, Gas Mark 4

Storage time
4–6 months

Defrosting time
6 hours at room temperature

225 g/8 oz ox liver
50 g/2 oz butter
450 g/1 lb cooked hare or rabbit, boned
4 thick rashers streaky bacon
2 cloves garlic, crushed
salt and pepper
1 tablespoon fine oatmeal
2 tablespoons whisky
2 teaspoons dried rosemary
2 bay leaves

Cut the liver into large pieces. Melt the butter and use to cook the liver lightly, until just firm. Allow to cool. Mince the liver with the cooked game meat. Derind and finely dice the bacon, or mince with the meats for a finer texture.

Mix all the ingredients together, except the bay leaves, including the butter used to cook the liver. Press the mixture into a greased terrine and smooth the top. Press the bay leaves on top of the pâté.

Cover with a lid or foil and cook in a moderate oven for about 1 hour. Cool.

To freeze: Cover the lid and secure with freezer tape. Label.
To serve: Defrost while still sealed. Serve with oatcakes and butter.
Serves 4–6

FREEZING HINT

Chicken giblets (minus livers) are cheap to buy separately and combine with the giblets from cooking a frozen chicken to make the basis for a hearty soup. Strain off the giblets and save the boneless bits for your pets.

FREEZING HINT

When freezing game birds, hang them for one day less than usual before plucking, drawing and freezing, to allow for further maturing during the defrosting time. Save the tail feathers if available and use these to garnish the bird after roasting.

13 Walnut cheese ball

Fennel with 14 mushroom dressing

You will need . . .

Storage time
4–6 months

Defrosting time
8 hours in the refrigerator

225 g/8 oz cream cheese
1½ teaspoons garlic or celery salt
1 tablespoon chopped parsley
1 tablespoon grated onion
1 tablespoon chopped green pepper
100 g/4 oz drained canned crushed
    pineapple
100 g/4 oz walnuts, chopped
When serving:
lettuce leaves
cocktail biscuits
olives
tomatoes

Beat the cream cheese until soft then gradually stir in the salt, parsley, onion, green pepper and crushed pineapple. Finally add half the nuts and combine well.

Chill in the refrigerator until firm.

Sprinkle the remaining nuts on a sheet of foil. Shape the chilled mixture into a ball and roll evenly in the nuts to coat.

To freeze: Wrap closely in foil, keeping the ball as round as possible. Seal and label.
To serve: Unwrap and place on a serving dish to defrost. Serve on lettuce leaves with small cocktail biscuits, olives and tomatoes.
Serves 4

You will need . . .

Cooking time
20 minutes

Storage time
4–6 months

Defrosting time
8 hours in the refrigerator

2 small bulbs fennel
1 tablespoon lemon juice
For the dressing:
100 g/4 oz button mushrooms
4 spring onions, trimmed
2 tablespoons lemon juice
½ teaspoon salt
¼ teaspoon pepper
1 teaspoon mild mustard
4 tablespoons oil
When serving:
4 tablespoons single cream
1 tablespoon chopped mint

First make the dressing. Thinly slice the mushrooms and chop the onions. Whisk together the lemon juice, salt, pepper, mustard and oil. Add the mushrooms and onions and refrigerate in a sealed container for 2 hours, turning once.

Cut the fennel bulbs in quarters and cook in lightly salted boiling water with the lemon juice for about 20 minutes, until just tender. Drain and cool.

Place in a polythene container and pour over the dressing.

To freeze: Cover surface with cling film. Seal and label.
To serve: Defrost while still sealed in the pack. Lift out the fennel quarters and divide among 4 small serving plates. Whisk the cream into the dressing and pour over the fennel. Sprinkle with chopped mint and serve cold.
Serves 4

FREEZING HINT

Fix a time to defrost and sort out your freezer when stocks are low. After the Christmas festivities or a big party is usually a good time — especially in cold weather.

FREEZING HINT

If you are doubtful how much freezer space to allocate to home grown vegetables, remember that some root vegetables keep well in the ground and need not be harvested until spring, so you can save space on these. Jerusalem artichokes are a good example.

Prawns with
15 curried mayonnaise

You will need . . .

225 g/8 oz peeled prawns
flour for coating
oil for frying
For the batter:
100 g/4 oz self-raising flour
pinch salt
150 ml/¼ pint water
When serving:
oil for frying
150 ml/¼ pint mayonnaise
1 teaspoon curry powder

Cooking time
6 minutes

Storage time
2–3 months

Defrosting
Reheat from frozen in hot oil

First make the batter. Sift the flour and salt into a bowl and beat in the water until smooth. Allow to stand while you prepare the prawns.

Dry them well with kitchen paper then coat with flour. Dip the coated prawns in the batter and fry a few at a time in deep hot oil for 2 minutes, until crisp and golden. Drain well on kitchen paper. Cool.

To freeze: Pack in a rigid container. Seal and label.
To serve: Refry from frozen in deep hot oil for 3 minutes. Meanwhile, beat the curry powder into the mayonnaise and hand separately.
Serves 4

FREEZING HINT

Square box-like shapes store in the freezer more tidily than round unevenly filled bags. Gussetted bags placed in a square rigid container produce ideal shapes when sealed with a twist tie and the same set of containers can be used repeatedly.

16 Poireaux provençale

You will need . . .

1 lemon
6 thin leeks
2 tablespoons olive oil
225 g/8 oz tomatoes
8 black olives
salt and pepper
When serving:
2 tablespoons olive oil
1 clove garlic, crushed
2 slices white bread, cubed

Cooking time
20 minutes

Storage time
4–6 months

Defrosting time
20 minutes in a pan of boiling water

Pare a long strip of rind from the lemon, and squeeze the juice. Trim the leeks, leaving only the white parts, and cut into 2.5-cm/1-inch rings. Wash well and drain.

Heat the oil, add the leeks and stir, cover the pan and cook gently for 10 minutes. Pour boiling water over the tomatoes, allow to stand for 1 minute, then drain and skin. Quarter the tomatoes, add to the leeks with the lemon juice, olives, salt and pepper to taste, and the strip of lemon rind. Cook for a further 10 minutes, uncovered. Cool and remove lemon rind.

To freeze: Pack in a boiling bag. Seal and label.
To serve: Place the bag in a pan of boiling water and reheat for 20 minutes. Meanwhile heat the oil with the crushed garlic and use to fry the bread cubes until golden brown. Drain. Serve portions sprinkled with these hot garlic croûtons.
Serves 4

FREEZING HINT

In summer this makes a lovely starter served chilled with cold garlic croûtons, also made in advance and frozen for a short period. If preferred, sprinkle plain croûtons with garlic salt.

17 Lemon tuna mousse

You will need . . .

Storage time
3–4 months

Defrosting time
6 hours at room
temperature or
8 hours in the refrigerator

1½ packets lemon jelly
450 ml/¾ pint boiling water
3 tablespoons vinegar
2 tablespoons grated onion
1 (198-g/7-oz) can tuna, drained
4 tablespoons finely chopped green
    pepper
20 stuffed green olives, chopped
½ teaspoon salt
300 ml/½ pint double cream, whipped
2 egg whites
When serving:
16 stuffed green olives
watercress

Dissolve the jelly in the boiling water, add the vinegar and onion and chill until syrupy.

Flake the tuna finely. Combine with the chopped green pepper, olives and salt and stir into the jelly mixture. Fold in the whipped cream. Whisk the egg whites until stiff and fold in gently, until well blended.

Quickly spoon into a 1.5-litre/2½-pint rigid polythene mould and smooth the top.

To freeze: Cover with foil or cling film. Seal and label.
To serve: Uncover to defrost. Turn mousse out of the mould and garnish with sliced olives and watercress.
Serves 6–8

Mackerel and 18 horseradish cream

You will need . . .

Storage time
3–4 months

Defrosting time
4 hours at room
temperature or
6 hours in the refrigerator

175 g/6 oz skinned smoked mackerel
50 g/2 oz butter
50 g/2 oz cream cheese
1 tablespoon creamed horseradish sauce
salt and pepper
2 tablespoons lemon juice
2 tablespoons single cream
When serving:
lemon wedges
black olives
parsley
hot toast

Carefully remove any bones from the mackerel. Blend the fish in a liquidiser with the softened butter, cream cheese, horseradish sauce, seasoning and lemon juice. Stir in the cream. (For a rougher textured pâté, simply mash all the ingredients together with a fork and beat well.) Taste and adjust for seasoning. Turn into individual ramekin dishes.

To freeze: Cover each ramekin with a cap of foil, well smoothed down the sides. Seal and label.
To serve: Defrost, and serve the ramekins on small plates, with lemon wedges, black olives, parsley and fingers of hot toast.
Serves 4

FREEZING HINT

If you possess a fish mould, use this for the mousse. Turn out when defrosted and surround the base with overlapping thin lemon slices.

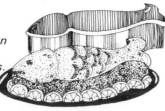

FREEZING HINT

Plant catchcrops of lettuce between rows of onions and dwarf peas. If the lettuces tend to 'bolt', use the hearts for salads and the outer leaves with onion thinnings and peas to make French pea soup for freezing.

19 Rich tomato mousse

You will need . . .

Cooking time
10 minutes

Storage time
4–6 months

Defrosting time
8 hours in the refrigerator

25 g/1 oz butter
1 small onion, chopped
50 g/2 oz mushrooms, sliced
650 ml/22 fl oz tomato juice
pinch ground cloves
pinch dried tarragon
1 teaspoon sugar
salt
few drops Tabasco sauce
15 g/½ oz gelatine
150 ml/¼ pint evaporated milk
1 tablespoon lemon juice
When serving:
lemon twist
sprig of parsley

Melt the butter and fry the onion and mushrooms gently until soft. Add the tomato juice, cloves, tarragon, sugar and salt to taste. Bring to the boil and simmer for 5 minutes.

Blend in a liquidiser or press through a sieve. Add the Tabasco. Dissolve the gelatine in 2 tablespoons water in a basin over a pan of hot water. Stir into the tomato mixture and cool.

Whisk the evaporated milk with the lemon juice until thick. Gradually whisk in the tomato mixture. Pour into an oiled mould and allow to set.

To freeze: Cover with foil and smooth down the sides. Label.
To serve: Uncover to defrost. Turn out and garnish with a lemon twist and parsley.
Serves 4

FREEZING HINT

Candles burn more slowly and evenly without 'tears' of wax running down the sides, if you put them in the freezer for 3 hours before lighting.

20 Little cheese soufflés

You will need . . .

Cooking time
10 minutes

Storage time
3 months

Defrosting time
2 hours at room temperature or
4 hours in the refrigerator

25 g/1 oz butter
1 generous tablespoon flour
150 ml/¼ pint milk
½ teaspoon made mustard
½ teaspoon salt
pinch cayenne pepper
75 g/3 oz cheese, grated
4 egg yolks
3 egg whites

Melt the butter in a small saucepan, stir in the flour and cook for 2 minutes over moderate heat. Add the milk, continue cooking until thick and smooth, stirring. Stir in the made mustard, seasonings and the grated cheese. When the cheese is almost completely melted, remove from the heat and beat in the egg yolks. Return to the heat, stirring constantly, for 1 minute. Turn into a fairly large bowl and cool.

Beat the egg whites until stiff and glossy, then fold into the cheese mixture, taking care to mix them through evenly. Spoon lightly into 4 individual soufflé dishes, piling up in the centres. Place together on a baking sheet.

To freeze: Open freeze until firm, then pack together in a polythene container, or place each on a square of foil, and fold up the points to cover the soufflés, and protect the surface if it is higher than the sides of the dishes.
To serve: Defrost and serve on small plates with brown bread rolls and butter.
Serves 4

FREEZING HINT

Whole eggs can be frozen provided they are removed from their shells and then lightly mixed with a fork. Stir in 1 teaspoon salt or 1½ teaspoons sugar to each 5 eggs and pack leaving a headspace. Label the pack whether for savoury or sweet use.

Easy economy recipes

Here is a glorious choice of recipes using pasta, pizza and rice as a basis, all easy to make and extremely economical. A richly flavoured sauce can turn a simple pasta dish into an excellent meal, and a tasty topping does the same for pizza. Rice has only recently come into its own as the basis of a main dish, but it is now an indispensable alternative to the former favourite, potatoes. Although of course there is still a place in the freezer for tasty economical potato dishes like these I have chosen.

Super sausage recipes and a selection of others, all chosen to be budget wise, make up this group of tempting freezables which are easy on the purse.

22 Seafood lasagne

21 Party pasta bake

(illustrated on back of jacket)

You will need . . .

Cooking time
about 50 minutes

Oven setting
190°C, 375°F, Gas Mark 5

Storage time
4–6 months

Defrosting time
4 hours in the refrigerator and 20 minutes in the oven

100 g/4 oz butter
3 tablespoons flour
450 ml/¾ pint milk
salt and pepper
1 onion, grated
6 rashers bacon, derinded
75 g/3 oz button mushrooms, sliced
225 g/8 oz shortcut macaroni, cooked
100 g/4 oz cheese, grated
When serving:
watercress

Melt half the butter and stir in the flour. Blend in the milk and season. Cook, stirring, until the sauce thickens. Add the onion. Chop 3 bacon rashers and fry with the mushrooms in the remaining butter. Cut the rest of the bacon into strips.

Stir the macaroni, fried bacon and mushrooms, and half the cheese into the sauce. Spoon into a foil container, top with the remaining cheese and the bacon strips. Cook in a moderately hot oven for 30 minutes. Cool.

To freeze: Cover with lid or foil. Seal and label.
To serve: Uncover to defrost, then reheat in a moderately hot oven for 20 minutes. Garnish with watercress, if liked.
Serves 4–6

You will need . . .

Cooking time
about 1 hour

Oven setting
180°C, 350°F, Gas Mark 4

Storage time
2–3 months

Defrosting time
4 hours in the refrigerator and 20 minutes in the oven

50 g/2 oz butter
1 onion, chopped
1 (396-g/14-oz) can tomatoes
2 tablespoons tomato purée
1 clove garlic, crushed
300 ml/½ pint red wine
salt and pepper
100 g/4 oz peeled prawns
100 g/4 oz shelled mussels
2 tablespoons chopped parsley
175 g/6 oz lasagne
50 g/2 oz Parmesan cheese, grated

Melt the butter and use to fry the onion gently for 5 minutes. Stir in the canned tomatoes, tomato purée, garlic, red wine and seasoning. Cook gently for 10 minutes then add the prawns, mussels and parsley.

Layer the dry lasagne and the seafood sauce in a foil-lined ovenproof dish or foil container, starting and finishing with a layer of sauce. Sprinkle over the Parmesan cheese.

Cook in a moderate oven for 45 minutes. Cool.

To freeze: Cover with lid or foil. Seal and label.
To serve: Uncover to defrost, then reheat in a moderate oven for 20 minutes.
Serves 4–6

FREEZING HINT

Cooked pasta can be frozen if a little oil is stirred into it while still hot. This keeps the strands separate. Pack in a polythene bag and reheat by turning out into a pan of boiling water and just returning to the boil.

FREEZING HINT

The lasagne can be assembled and frozen before cooking. When required, cook from frozen in a moderate oven for 1 hour.

Cannelloni
23 with chicken livers

24 Chilli beef

You will need . . .

Cooking time
55 minutes

Oven setting
180°C, 350°F, Gas Mark 4

Storage time
6–9 months

Defrosting time
4 hours in the refrigerator
and 30 minutes in the oven

225 g/8 oz cannelloni
225 g/8 oz chicken livers
1 onion, finely chopped
3 tablespoons oil
50 g/2 oz mushrooms, chopped
1 egg, beaten
2 tablespoons savoury stuffing mix
salt and pepper
3 tablespoons single cream
300 ml/½ pint whisked savoury sauce
  (see recipe 210)
50 g/2 oz cheese, grated
When serving:
tomato slices
sprigs of watercress

You will need . . .

Cooking time
1¾ hours

Oven setting
180°C, 350°F, Gas Mark 4

Storage time
4–6 months

Defrosting time
4 hours in the refrigerator
and 40 minutes in the oven

2 onions, sliced
3 tablespoons oil
600 g/1¼ lb lean stewing steak, trimmed
seasoned flour
1 tablespoon mild chilli powder
2 tablespoons tomato purée
1 (396-g/14-oz) can tomatoes
600 ml/1 pint beef stock
salt and pepper
100 g/4 oz pasta shells

Cook the cannelloni in boiling salted water for 8 minutes, until just tender. Drain thoroughly.

Meanwhile, chop the chicken livers and fry with the onion in the oil for 10 minutes. Add the mushrooms and cook for 5 minutes. Stir in the beaten egg, stuffing mix and seasoning to taste.

Split each tube of cannelloni lengthwise, fill with the meat mixture and roll up. Arrange in a greased foil container. Stir the cream into the sauce, spoon over the cannelloni and sprinkle with the cheese. Bake in a moderate oven for 30 minutes. Cool.

To freeze: Cover with lid or foil. Seal and label.
To serve: Uncover to defrost, then reheat in a moderate oven for 30 minutes. Serve garnished with tomato slices and sprigs of watercress.
Serves 4

Fry the onion gently in the oil for 5 minutes. Cut the steak into cubes and toss in seasoned flour. Add to the pan and fry gently, turning frequently until sealed on all sides.

Stir in the chilli powder, tomato purée, canned tomatoes and stock. Bring to the boil and cover the pan. Simmer for 1½ hours. Taste and adjust the seasoning if necessary. Add the dry pasta shells to the meat mixture and allow to cool. (If you are eating the dish immediately, add the pasta shells and simmer for a further 20 minutes.)

To freeze: Pack in a foil container. Seal and label.
To serve: Defrost and then reheat in a moderate oven for 40 minutes.
Serves 4

FREEZING HINT

The cannelloni can be cooked, stuffed and coated with sauce then frozen before baking. When required, cook from frozen in a moderate oven for 1 hour.

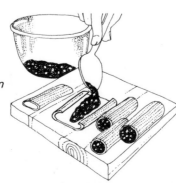

FREEZING HINT

When preparing a large quantity of diced meat for a casserole cook-in, reserve all the trimmings and boil up to make good strong stock. Freeze in ice cube trays then pack the cubes in polythene bags.

25 Sausage and ale pie

You will need . . .

Cooking time
30 minutes

Oven setting
200°C, 400°F, Gas Mark 6

Storage time
3–4 months

Defrosting time
50 minutes in the oven from frozen

50 g/2 oz fat
450 g/1 lb large pork sausages
100 g/4 oz baby onions, peeled
40 g/1½ oz flour
450 ml/¾ pint brown ale
salt and pepper
100 g/4 oz button mushrooms
225 g/8 oz puff pastry
When serving:
beaten egg to glaze
sprig of parsley

Melt the fat and fry the sausages gently for about 8 minutes, until pale golden. Place in a large pie dish or foil container. Add the onions to the fat in the pan and fry until golden. Spoon over the sausages.

Stir the flour into the remaining pan fat and cook for 3 minutes. Gradually stir in the brown ale and season to taste. Bring to the boil, stirring constantly, add the mushrooms and pour over the sausages.

Roll out the pastry and cut a lid to cover the pie filling. Dampen the edges to seal, decorate with pastry trimmings and mark a criss-cross pattern with a knife.

To freeze: Open freeze until solid. Cover with foil. Seal and label.
To serve: Uncover and brush with beaten egg. Cook from frozen in a moderately hot oven for 50 minutes, and serve garnished with parsley.
Serves 6

FREEZING HINT

Tiny pickling onions are available for only a short period each year. Peel and blanch them in boiling water for 7 minutes, then freeze in a creamy white sauce seasoned with nutmeg and black pepper.

26 Sausage and onion toad

You will need . . .

Cooking time
15 minutes

Oven setting
220°C, 425°F, Gas Mark 7

Storage time
3–4 months

Defrosting time
45 minutes in the oven from frozen

25 g/1 oz fat
450 g/1 lb large beef sausages
100 g/4 oz plain flour
pinch salt
1 teaspoon dry mustard
1 teaspoon dried mixed herbs
1 small onion, grated
1 egg
300 ml/½ pint milk

Place the fat in a shallow ovenproof dish or foil container and melt in a hot oven. Put in the sausages, return to the oven and cook for 10 minutes. Allow to become quite cold.

To make the batter, sift the flour, salt and mustard into a bowl. Beat in the herbs, grated onion, egg and a little of the milk. Gradually beat in the remaining milk to give a smooth batter.

Arrange the sausages evenly in the dish and pour over the batter.

To freeze: Open freeze until solid. Cover with lid or foil. Seal and label.
To serve: Uncover and cook from frozen in a hot oven for 45 minutes.
Serves 4–6
Note: This can also be made in individual foil containers.

FREEZING HINT

To grate an onion without discomfort, peel it well ahead of time. Wrap in foil and freeze for at least 2 hours before grating.

Sausages
27 in mustard sauce

You will need . . .

Cooking time
about 40 minutes

Oven setting
190°C, 375°F, Gas Mark 5

Storage time
3–4 months

Defrosting time
4 hours in the refrigerator
and 30 minutes in the oven

4 Cumberland sausages
4 thick rashers lean bacon
2 tablespoons oil
1 onion, sliced
1 tablespoon fine breadcrumbs
600 ml/1 pint whisked savoury sauce
 (see recipe 210)
1 tablespoon French mustard
juice ½ lemon
1 tablespoon sugar
100 g/4 oz button mushrooms, sliced
salt and pepper

Wrap each sausage in a rasher of bacon and secure with a wooden cocktail stick. Grill for 5 minutes on each side.

Heat the oil in a shallow pan and use to fry the onion gently for 3 minutes. Stir in the breadcrumbs. Add the savoury sauce, French mustard, lemon juice, sugar, mushrooms and seasoning. Bring to the boil, stirring all the time, and add the bacon and sausage rolls.

Cover and simmer for 20 minutes. Remove the cocktail sticks and cool.

To freeze: Pack in a foil container. Seal and label.
To serve: Uncover to defrost then reheat in a moderately hot oven for 30 minutes. Serve garnished with tomato slices and parsley, accompanied by a side salad, if liked.
Serves 4
Note: Large pork or beef sausages could be used instead of Cumberland sausages.

FREEZING HINT

A time-saving tip when you serve roast pork is to defrost some apple slices, and toss the cooked vegetables to accompany the joint in butter with the apple slices. This combines vegetables and apple sauce together.

Sweet-sour
28 sausage loaf

You will need . . .

Cooking time
55 minutes

Oven setting
190°C, 375°F, Gas Mark 5

Storage time
3–4 months

Defrosting time
2 hours in the refrigerator
and 30 minutes in the oven

6 rashers streaky bacon
450 g/1 lb pork sausagemeat
1 onion, finely chopped
25 g/1 oz breadcrumbs
1 teaspoon dried mixed herbs
1 tablespoon Worcestershire sauce
salt and pepper
2 eggs, beaten
1 (396-g/14-oz) can tomatoes
1 tablespoon tomato purée
juice 1 lemon
50 g/2 oz soft brown sugar

Chop 2 of the bacon rashers. Mix the sausagemeat with the chopped bacon and onion, the breadcrumbs, herbs, Worcestershire sauce, seasoning and beaten eggs.

Line a loaf tin with the remaining bacon rashers, halved and stretched, and press in the sausagemeat mixture. Cover with greased paper and bake in a moderately hot oven for 45 minutes. Cool.

Meanwhile, make the sauce. Simmer the tomatoes and their juice with the tomato purée, lemon juice, brown sugar and seasoning to taste, for 5 minutes. Cool.

To freeze: Remove loaf from tin and pack in foil or a polythene bag. Freeze sauce in a polythene container. Seal and label.
To serve: Unwrap the loaf and place in an ovenproof dish to defrost. Pour the sauce around the loaf and reheat in a moderately hot oven for 30 minutes. Serve garnished with watercress, if liked.
Serves 4–6

FREEZING HINT

When collecting leftover red wine to freeze, always pour through a fine sieve, as there is frequently sediment at the bottom of the bottle.

29 Pizza al salami

You will need . . .

Cooking time
30 minutes

Oven setting
220°C, 425°F, Gas Mark 7

Storage time
3—4 months

Defrosting time
2 hours in the refrigerator
and 10 minutes in the oven

¼ teaspoon sugar
150 ml/¼ pint warm water
1½ teaspoons dried yeast
225 g/8 oz plain flour
½ teaspoon salt
15 g/½ oz butter
olive oil
4 tomatoes, sliced
1 clove garlic, crushed
1 tablespoon tomato purée
4 tablespoons red wine
50 g/2 oz salami, chopped
100 g/4 oz cheese

To make the dough, dissolve the sugar in the water and sprinkle the yeast on top. Leave in a warm place for 10 minutes until frothy.

Sift the flour and salt into a bowl and rub in the butter. Mix to a dough with the yeast liquid. Knead until smooth. Put into an oiled bowl, cover with greased polythene and leave in a warm place until doubled in size. Knead again until smooth.

Roll the dough out to a circle 5 mm/¼ inch thick and place on a greased baking tray. Brush with oil and top with tomato slices. Mix together the garlic, tomato purée and wine and spoon over. Add the salami and thinly sliced cheese and sprinkle with a little extra oil. Bake in a hot oven for 30 minutes. Cool.

To freeze: Pack in foil or a polythene bag. Seal and label.
To serve: Unwrap to defrost then reheat in a hot oven for 10 minutes. Garnish with a sprig of parsley.
Serves 2—3

FREEZING HINT

Pizza can be frozen uncooked. When required to serve, uncover, place on a baking tray and cook from frozen in a hot oven for about 40 minutes.

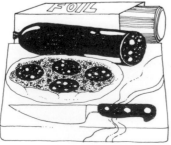

30 Breakfast pizza

You will need . . .

Cooking time
35—40 minutes

Oven setting
220°C, 425°F, Gas Mark 7

Storage time
3—4 months

Defrosting time
2 hours in the refrigerator
and 10 minutes in the oven

1 quantity basic pizza dough
  (see recipe 29)
50 g/2 oz butter
100 g/4 oz mushrooms, sliced
olive oil
4 chipolata sausages
4 rashers bacon
50 g/2 oz cheese, grated
2 tablespoons chopped parsley
salt and pepper

Roll the pizza dough to a circle 5 mm/¼ inch thick, and place on an oiled baking tray.

Melt the butter and fry the mushrooms gently for 5 minutes. Brush the pizza base with oil and cover with the mushrooms. Cut the sausages into chunks. Derind and cut the bacon into strips. Top the pizza with the chunks of sausage, grated cheese, parsley and seasoning. Arrange the bacon strips to make a lattice over the top of the pizza.

Sprinkle over a little extra oil and bake in a hot oven for 30 minutes. Cool.

To freeze: Pack in foil or a polythene bag. Seal and label.
To serve: Unwrap to defrost then reheat in a hot oven for 10 minutes.
Serves 2—3

FREEZING HINT

To make breakfast for four people, cut the cooked pizza into quarters and top each with a poached or scrambled egg.

31 Seafood pizza

You will need . . .

Cooking time
35 minutes

Oven setting
220°C, 425°F, Gas Mark 7

Storage time
2–3 months

Defrosting time
2 hours in the refrigerator
and 10 minutes in the oven

1 quantity basic pizza dough
   (see recipe 29)
1 onion
olive oil
1 (396-g/14-oz) can tomatoes, drained
1 tablespoon tomato purée
100 g/4 oz canned tuna, flaked
75 g/3 oz peeled prawns
6 anchovy fillets, chopped
pepper
75 g/3 oz cheese, grated
When serving:
parsley

Roll the pizza dough to a circle 5 mm/$\frac{1}{4}$ inch thick and place on an oiled baking tray.

Finely chop the onion and fry gently in a little olive oil for 5 minutes. Drain and mix with the tomatoes, tomato purée, tuna, prawns, chopped anchovies and pepper to taste. Brush the pizza base with oil and top with the tomato seafood mixture.

Sprinkle the pizza with the grated cheese and a little extra oil and bake in a hot oven for 30 minutes. Cool.

To freeze: Pack in foil or a polythene bag. Seal and label.
To serve: Unwrap to defrost then reheat in a hot oven for 10 minutes. Serve garnished with parsley.
Serves 2–3

FREEZING HINT

For a more economical version of this pizza, substitute a can of pilchards, boned and mashed, for the tomato seafood.

32 Fruit pizza

You will need . . .

Cooking time
30 minutes

Oven setting
220°C, 425°F, Gas Mark 7

Storage time
3–4 months

Defrosting time
2 hours in the refrigerator
and 10 minutes in the oven

1 quantity basic pizza dough
   (see recipe 29)
50 g/2 oz butter, melted
6 tablespoons apricot jam, melted
2 red-skinned apples, sliced
1 (227-g/8-oz) can pineapple chunks,
   drained
50 g/2 oz flaked almonds

Roll the pizza dough to a circle 5 mm/$\frac{1}{4}$ inch thick and place on an oiled baking tray.

Brush with half the melted butter and a little of the apricot jam. Arrange overlapping slices of apple around the edge and pineapple chunks in the centre. Spoon over the remaining apricot jam and sprinkle a border of flaked almonds.

Trickle over the rest of the melted butter and bake in a hot oven for 30 minutes. Cool.

To freeze: Pack in foil or a polythene bag. Seal and label.
To serve: Unwrap to defrost then reheat in a hot oven for 10 minutes. Serve hot with cream or custard, if liked.
Serves 3–4

FREEZING HINT

To make a change, substitute a can of fruit salad for the apple and pineapple. Drain and use as above.

33 Red bean chowder

New England
34 fish chowder

You will need . . .

225 g/8 oz red kidney beans
1 litre/1¾ pints water
salt and pepper
2 large carrots
1 large onion
1 green pepper
1 (396-g/14-oz) can tomatoes
1 tablespoon cornflour
250 ml/8 fl oz milk

Cooking time
2¼ hours

Storage time
4–6 months

Defrosting
Reheat from frozen in a
saucepan

You will need . . .

225 g/8 oz salt belly of pork, diced
1 large onion, sliced
450 g/1 lb cod fillet
450 g/1 lb potatoes, diced
300 ml/½ pint milk
¼ teaspoon pepper
½ teaspoon celery salt
When serving:
25 g/1 oz butter
salt and pepper

Cooking time
about 30 minutes

Storage time
4–6 months

Defrosting time
6 hours at room temperature
then reheat in a saucepan

Rinse the beans and soak in the water overnight. Add salt
and bring to the boil. Cover and simmer for 1 hour.

Dice the carrots, chop the onion and deseed and dice
the green pepper. Add the vegetables to the beans with
the tomatoes and their liquid. Simmer for 30 minutes.

Moisten the cornflour with a little cold water, add to the
chowder and stir until boiling. Simmer for a further 30
minutes, until very thick. Stir in the milk and adjust the
seasoning. Cool.

To freeze: Pack in a polythene container. Seal and label.
To serve: Turn frozen chowder into a saucepan, add 4
tablespoons water and reheat gently to boiling point,
stirring frequently.
Serves 4

Gently fry the diced pork until the fat begins to run. Add
the onion and cook for a further 5 minutes.

Cut the cod into chunks and add to the pan with the
potato, milk and seasonings.

Cover the pan and cook gently for about 15 minutes,
until the fish and potatoes are tender. Cool.

To freeze: Pack in a polythene container or foil or
polythene-lined carton. Seal and label.
To serve: Defrost while still sealed in the pack. Turn the
chowder into a saucepan and reheat gently to boiling
point. Stir frequently but gently to avoid breaking down
the fish and potatoes. Stir in the butter and adjust the
seasoning.
Serves 4

FREEZING HINT

*A large quantity of leftover wine
can be boiled to concentrate it and
drive off the alcohol, so that it
need not be added until the end of
cooking time, and still gives
plenty of flavour to the dish.*

FREEZING HINT

*When using polythene containers
for which the lid forms a seal,
always close firmly, and lift one
corner, or part of the round edge,
just to expel surplus air and create
a vacuum when you seal.*

Quick
35 barbecued spareribs

You will need . . .

Cooking time
10 minutes

Storage time
4–6 months

Defrosting time
4 hours at room temperature
and 25 minutes under the
grill

1 kg/2¼ lb meaty pork spareribs
For the sauce:
250 ml/8 fl oz water
1 chicken stock cube, crumbled
75 g/3 oz golden syrup
1 clove garlic, crushed
pinch ground ginger
pinch ground cinnamon
3 tablespoons soy sauce
2 tablespoons tomato ketchup
2 teaspoons tomato purée

Place the spareribs in a roasting tin or baking dish.
    Mix together all the ingredients for the sauce and bring
to the boil, stirring constantly.
    Pour the sauce over the spareribs and cool.

To freeze: Cover with foil or polythene. Seal and label.
To serve: Uncover to defrost then place the dish of spareribs under a hot grill and cook for 15 minutes, basting and
turning several times. Drain the sauce into a pan and boil
hard to reduce until syrupy. Continue to grill the ribs for a
further 10 minutes until they brown and the edges become
crisp. Place in a hot serving dish and pour the thickened
sauce over the top. Serve with fluffy boiled rice.
Serves 4

FREEZING HINT

*To make a starter for a party meal
the quantity of spareribs in the
above recipe will serve 8 without
the rice as an accompaniment. Put
finger bowls on the table or hand
round tissues.*

Bacon
36 and split pea stew

You will need . . .

Cooking time
about 1¾ hours

Storage time
3–4 months

Defrosting time
4 hours in the refrigerator
then reheat in a saucepan

175 g/6 oz dried split peas
small knuckle green bacon
50 g/2 oz butter
2 onions, chopped
2 carrots, chopped
generous litre/2 pints chicken stock
chopped parsley
pepper
3 frankfurter sausages, halved

Soak the peas and the knuckle of bacon separately overnight in cold water. Drain both thoroughly.
    Melt the butter and use to fry the chopped onion and
carrot gently for 5 minutes. Add the split peas, knuckle of
bacon, chicken stock, parsley and pepper to taste. Bring
to the boil then reduce the heat and simmer for 1½ hours.
    Remove the knuckle of bacon, take off any meat and
chop. Add the chopped bacon and halved frankfurters to
the stew. Cool.

To freeze: Pack in a polythene container. Seal and label.
To serve: Uncover to defrost then turn into a saucepan
and bring slowly to the boil. Simmer for 5 minutes.
Serves 4

FREEZING HINT

*A good way to remove excess fat
from soup or stew is to chill it until
the fat solidifies on top, then
scoop it off with a slotted spoon.*

37 Sweetcorn risotto

You will need . . .

Cooking time
40–45 minutes

Oven setting
190°C, 375°F, Gas Mark 5

Storage time
4–6 months

Defrosting time
3 hours in the refrigerator
and 25 minutes in the oven

50 g/2 oz butter
2 rashers streaky bacon, chopped
1 small onion
1 (198-g/7-oz) can sweetcorn, drained
600 ml/1 pint chicken stock
225 g/8 oz long-grain rice
2 tablespoons chopped parsley
75 g/3 oz Parmesan cheese, grated
salt and pepper
When serving:
chopped parsley

Melt the butter and use to fry the bacon slowly until the fat
runs. Finely chop the onion, add to the pan and fry gently
for 5 minutes. Add the sweetcorn and half the stock.
Cover and simmer for 10 minutes. Add the rice and
gradually stir in the rest of the stock.

Bring to the boil and allow to simmer for about 20
minutes, stirring occasionally with a fork, until most of the
liquid has been absorbed and the rice is just tender. Do
not overcook or the risotto will be mushy. Remove from
the heat, stir in the parsley, cheese and seasoning. Cool.

To freeze: Pack in a polythene or foil container. Seal and
label.
To serve: Uncover to defrost. Turn into an ovenproof
container and reheat in a moderately hot oven for 25 minutes. The rice tends to swell further and become softer
when the risotto is reheated. Serve sprinkled with parsley.
Serves 4

FREEZING HINT

*Parsley is a good herb for
continual use and makes a
decorative garden border. Sprigs
freeze well in small bags and can
be crumbled while still frozen to
avoid the chore of chopping.*

38 Rice moussaka

You will need . . .

Cooking time
30 minutes

Oven setting
190°C, 375°F, Gas Mark 5

Storage time
4–6 months

Defrosting time
45–50 minutes in the oven
from frozen

175 g/6 oz long-grain rice
2 tablespoons oil
1 onion, chopped
225 g/8 oz minced beef
1 tablespoon tomato purée
4 tomatoes, chopped
150 ml/¼ pint beef stock
salt and pepper
600 ml/1 pint whisked savoury sauce
  (see recipe 210)
100 g/4 oz cheese, grated

Cook the rice in boiling salted water until just tender.
Drain.

Meanwhile, heat the oil and fry the onion gently for a
few minutes. Add the minced beef and cook, stirring, until
browned. Add the tomato purée, chopped tomatoes and
stock. Season to taste and simmer for 15 minutes. Mix
the white sauce with the cooked rice and half the grated
cheese.

Spoon half the rice mixture into a foil container or
ovenproof dish and cover with the meat mixture. Top with
the remaining rice mixture and sprinkle with the rest of the
cheese. Cool.

To freeze: Cover with lid or foil. Seal and label.
To serve: Uncover and cook from frozen in a moderately
hot oven for 45–50 minutes. Serve garnished with
tomato slices and a sprig of parsley.
Serves 6

FREEZING HINT

*If you have limited garden space,
try planting outdoor tomatoes and
globe artichokes among the
flowers. Both are decorative and
provide useful crops for freezing.*

39 Rice and chicken cakes

You will need . . .

225 g/8 oz cooked long-grain rice
150 ml/¼ pint whisked savoury sauce
   (see recipe 210)
50 g/2 oz nuts, chopped
175 g/6 oz cooked chicken, chopped
50 g/2 oz sultanas
1 teaspoon curry powder
2 egg yolks
salt and pepper
flour
1 egg, beaten
toasted breadcrumbs
When serving:
lemon slices

Storage time
4–6 months

Defrosting time
15 minutes in hot oil from
frozen

Mix together the cooked rice, white sauce, nuts, chopped chicken, sultanas, curry powder and egg yolks. Season well with salt and a little pepper.

Form into 8 square cakes and chill for 2–3 hours.

Turn the cakes in flour, dip into beaten egg and coat with breadcrumbs, taking care the cakes are completely sealed.

To freeze: Open freeze until solid then pack in a polythene container with dividers. Seal and label.
To serve: Fry from frozen in hot oil for 15 minutes. Drain and serve hot with a sweet and sour sauce (see recipe 79) or with a green salad. Garnish with quartered lemon slices.
Serves 4

FREEZING HINT

When blanching vegetables for freezing, timing must be accurate from the moment the water comes back to the boil. Cool the vegetables in a bowl of iced water or under cold running water.

40 Spanish rice au gratin

You will need . . .

75 g/3 oz brown rice
300 ml/½ pint water
1 teaspoon salt
50 g/2 oz onion, chopped
25 g/1 oz green pepper, chopped
50 g/2 oz celery, chopped
15 g/½ oz butter
1 (227-g/8-oz) can tomatoes
1 teaspoon brown sugar
1 teaspoon mild chilli powder
4 black olives, stoned
100 g/4 oz processed cheese, grated

Cooking time
about 1 hour

Oven setting
190°C, 375°F, Gas Mark 5

Storage time
4–6 months

Defrosting time
6 hours at room temperature
and 30–35 minutes in the
oven

Combine the rice, water and salt. Bring to the boil, cover and simmer for 45 minutes.

Meanwhile, sauté the onion, pepper and celery in the butter until soft. Stir in the tomatoes and their liquid, the brown sugar and chilli powder. Add the cooked rice and simmer until thick, about 10 minutes.

Transfer the mixture to a greased foil container. Slice the olives and scatter on top. Sprinkle with the grated cheese and cool.

To freeze: Cover with lid. Seal and label.
To serve: Defrost at room temperature, then reheat in a moderately hot oven until heated through and the cheese is melted on top. Serve garnished with black olives and parsley, accompanied by a side salad if liked.
Serves 4
Note: If using white long-grain rice, reduce cooking times accordingly.

FREEZING HINT

Frozen ratatouille or vegetable mixtures can be turned into a main meal dish when defrosted. Spread the mixture in a shallow ovenproof dish, heat in the oven until piping hot, break eggs into dimples formed with the back of a spoon and bake until the eggs are set.

41 Crusty tuna pie

Cutlet
42 parcels with chutney

You will need . . .

Cooking time
about 40 minutes

Oven setting
190°C, 375°F, Gas Mark 5

Storage time
3–4 months

Defrosting time
4 hours at room temperature
and 20 minutes in the oven

1 medium onion
350 g/12 oz potato, grated
salt and pepper
50 g/2 oz butter
2 sticks celery, chopped
50 g/2 oz soft breadcrumbs
1 (198-g/7-oz) can tuna
1 egg, beaten
50 g/2 oz Cheddar cheese, grated

Grate half the onion, mix with the potato and add salt to taste. Pat the mixture into a greased foil container to make a thick shell. Build up the sides slightly. Melt three-quarters of the butter and sprinkle over the potato shell.

Finely chop the rest of the onion. Melt the remaining butter and fry the chopped onion and celery until soft. Stir in the breadcrumbs, flaked tuna and liquid from the can, the beaten egg and seasoning to taste. Spoon into the potato shell.

Cover lightly with foil and bake in a moderately hot oven for 35 minutes. Remove from the oven, sprinkle with the cheese and cool.

To freeze: Cover with lid or foil. Seal and label.
To serve: Uncover to defrost, then reheat in a moderately hot oven for 20 minutes.
Serves 4

You will need . . .

Cooking time
45 minutes

Oven setting
180°C, 350°F, Gas Mark 4

Storage time
4–6 months

Defrosting time
30 minutes in the oven
from frozen

12 lamb cutlets
6 medium potatoes, sliced
6 tablespoons chutney
salt and pepper

Trim the cutlets of any excess fat and place them in pairs on large squares of foil.

Divide the potatoes and chutney among the parcels and place on top of the cutlets. Season to taste.

Fold up the foil to close the parcels, place on a baking tray and cook in a moderate oven for 30 minutes, then open the parcels and cook for a further 15 minutes. Cool.

To freeze: Close the parcels and put together in a poly-thene container. Seal and label.
To serve: Place the frozen parcels on a baking tray and reheat in a moderate oven for 30 minutes. Serve with a green salad.
Serves 6

FREEZING HINT

To make a quick filling for savoury pancakes, combine equal quantities of frozen chopped spinach and frozen savoury white sauce. Stir them together over moderate heat until well combined.

FREEZING HINT

Pack small cuts of meat and chops with dividers so that they can be easily separated and the required number removed and cooked from the frozen state.

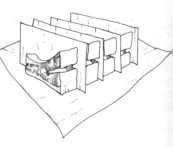

43 Herbed luncheon loaf

You will need . . .

Cooking time
45–50 minutes

Oven setting
180°C, 350°F, Gas Mark 4
190°C, 375°F, Gas Mark 5

Storage time
4–6 months

Defrosting time
35–40 minutes in the oven
from frozen

2 (439-g/15½-oz) cans butter beans
1 onion
1 egg
15 g/½ oz butter, melted
½ teaspoon salt
pinch pepper
¼ teaspoon dried sage
75 g/3 oz dry wholemeal breadcrumbs
75 g/3 oz chopped mixed nuts
2 tablespoons tomato purée
When serving:
watercress
tomato slices

Drain and mash the beans. Grate the onion and stir into the mashed beans with the remaining ingredients.

Spoon the mixture into a greased 1-kg/2-lb loaf tin and bake in a moderate oven for 45–50 minutes. Turn out and cool.

To freeze: Wrap in foil. Seal and label.
To serve: Reheat from frozen, still wrapped, in a moderately hot oven for 35–40 minutes. Serve sliced, garnished with sprigs of watercress and tomato slices.
Serves 4

FREEZING HINT

When freezing meat, remove as much excess fat as possible as this tends to go rancid and shorten the storage life of the meat. The fat can be made into dripping.

44 Potato ring pie

You will need . . .

Cooking time
about 50 minutes

Oven setting
200°C, 400°F, Gas Mark 6

Storage time
4–6 months

Defrosting time
4 hours at room temperature
and 40 minutes in the oven

50 g/2 oz butter
1 large onion, sliced
1 large carrot, diced
350 g/12 oz lean minced beef
pinch dried sage
250 ml/8 fl oz beef stock
1 tablespoon gravy powder
salt and pepper
2 tablespoons milk
675 g/1½ lb mashed potato
When serving:
1 (198-g/7-oz) can sweetcorn
50 g/2 oz frozen peas

Melt half the butter and gently fry the onion and carrot until golden. Add the beef and cook, stirring, until it changes colour. Add the sage with the blended stock and gravy powder and bring to the boil, stirring constantly. Cover and simmer for 30 minutes. Season to taste and place in an ovenproof dish, or individual gratin dishes.

Beat the remaining butter and the milk into the potato, then pipe or fork it around the meat mixture. Cool.

To freeze: Cover with lid and secure with freezer tape or cover with foil. Seal and label.
To serve: Uncover to defrost then reheat in a moderately hot oven for 40 minutes. Meanwhile, cook the sweetcorn and liquid from the can with the peas for 5 minutes. Drain and spoon the vegetables into the centre of the cooked pie.
Serves 4

FREEZING HINT

Frozen chips are a temptation to dieters, but you can enjoy them and limit the calorie intake by baking or grilling the chips dry, instead of frying. Allow double the frying time to get them really brown.

Cheerful casseroles

There is nothing like a hearty casserole meal to keep the family happy and well fed. The great joy of casserole cooking is that almost a whole meal is cooked in one dish, which means exact timing is not so important, and cheaper cuts of meat become tender and succulent with long slow cooking. To give you plenty to choose from, these recipes include your favourite meats; lamb, pork and beef, as well as chicken and game, and the less expensive varieties of fish.

Versatile vegetables can also make very tasty casseroles, as the four original dishes in this section show.

45 Lamb with lentils

(illustrated on back of jacket)

You will need . . .

Cooking time
1¾ hours

Storage time
4–6 months

Defrosting time
4 hours at room temperature then reheat in a saucepan

225 g/8 oz lentils
1 kg/2¼ lb neck of lamb chops
25 g/1 oz seasoned flour
1 tablespoon oil
600 ml/1 pint beef stock
600 ml/1 pint dry cider
1 large cooking apple, peeled
½ teaspoon dried sage
salt and pepper
When serving:
chopped parsley

Soak the lentils overnight, then drain. Trim the chops and coat with seasoned flour.

Heat the oil in a large saucepan and fry the chops for about 4 minutes until golden brown on both sides. Add the stock, drained lentils and cider and stir until the mixture come to the boil. Meanwhile, quarter the apple and cut each piece into 4 wedges. Add the apple and sage to the saucepan, cover and simmer for 1½ hours. Adjust for seasoning. Cool.

To freeze: Pack in a polythene container. Seal and label.
To serve: Defrost at room temperature, turn into a large saucepan and reheat slowly to boiling point, stirring. Simmer for 5 minutes and serve garnished with parsley.
Serves 4

Marinated 46 lamb casserole

You will need . . .

Cooking time
about 2¼ hours

Oven setting
160°C, 325°F, Gas Mark 3

Storage time
4–6 months

Defrosting time
6–8 hours in the refrigerator then reheat in a saucepan

675 g/1½ lb middle neck lamb
grated zest of 1 lemon
1 tablespoon chopped mint
1 tablespoon soft brown sugar
2 tablespoons vinegar
salt and pepper
seasoned flour
2 tablespoons oil
25 g/1 oz butter
750 ml/1¼ pints stock
2 medium potatoes, diced
100 g/4 oz button onions
100 g/4 oz button mushrooms

Cut the lamb into large pieces and place in a shallow dish with the lemon zest, mint, sugar, vinegar and seasoning. Cover and chill for 1 hour, to marinate.

Drain the lamb pieces on kitchen paper and coat in seasoned flour. Heat the oil and butter and use to brown the lamb on all sides.

Put the lamb into a casserole dish. Add the stock, mint marinade, potato and button onions. Cover and cook for 2 hours in a moderate oven, adding the mushrooms for the last 15 minutes. Cool.

To freeze: Pack in a foil-lined casserole dish or polythene container. Seal and label.
To serve: Uncover to defrost, then turn into a saucepan, reheat to boiling point and simmer for 5 minutes.
Serves 4

FREEZING HINT

As a more unusual garnish to this dish, try thin wedges of dessert apple. These can be prepared up to 30 minutes in advance and will not discolour if placed in a small bowl of salted water until required.

FREEZING HINT

When cooking a large joint, prepare extra green vegetables, roast potatoes and gravy. Use these with a few slices of the meat to make up plate meals to pop into the freezer at very little extra trouble and expense.

47 Lamb with honey sauce

Noisettes
48 with tarragon sauce

You will need . . .

Cooking time
about 2–2½ hours

Oven setting
180°C, 350°F, Gas Mark 4

Storage time
4–6 months

Defrosting time
4 hours at room temperature
and 35 minutes in the oven

4 tablespoons flour
salt and pepper
1 kg/ 2¼ lb neck of lamb chops
2 tablespoons oil
8 pickled onions
225 g/8 oz carrots, sliced
100 g/4 oz frozen peas
225 g/8 oz new potatoes, scraped
1 litre/1¾ pints stock
2 tablespoons honey

You will need . . .

Cooking time
about 1½ hours

Oven setting
180°C, 350°F, Gas Mark 4

Storage time
4–6 months

Defrosting time
1 hour in the oven from
frozen

1 best end neck of lamb, boned
1 tablespoon oil
225 g/8 oz onions, sliced
300 ml/½ pint stock
2 teaspoons dried tarragon
salt and pepper
1 tablespoon cornflour
300 ml/½ pint milk
When serving:
parsley

Season the flour with salt and pepper and use some to coat the chops. Heat the oil in a frying pan, put in the floured chops and brown on both sides. Remove and place in an ovenproof casserole or foil container with the pickled onions, carrot slices, peas and potatoes.

Sprinkle any remaining flour into the fat in the frying pan and stir well. Gradually add the stock and bring to the boil, stirring constantly. Blend in the honey, season to taste with salt and pepper, and pour over the lamb and vegetables.

Cover and cook in a moderate oven for 1½–2 hours, until the meat is tender. Cool.

To freeze: Secure lid with freezer tape, or cover container with lid or foil. Seal and label.
To serve: Uncover to defrost, then reheat in a moderate oven for 35 minutes.
Serves 6

Roll and tie the boned best end. Heat the oil in a frying pan and use to seal the joint on all sides.

Transfer the meat to an ovenproof casserole and add the onion, stock, tarragon and salt and pepper. Cover and cook in a moderate oven for 1¼ hours. Remove the joint and slice thickly. Pour the meat stock into a saucepan. Moisten the cornflour with a little milk, add to the pan and bring to the boil, stirring all the time. Add the remaining milk and cool.

To freeze: Pack the meat slices and sauce in a foil container. Seal and label.
To serve: Uncover and place still frozen in a moderate oven for 1 hour. Serve garnished with parsley.
Serves 4

FREEZING HINT

When packing meat with bones, pad bone ends to avoid puncturing the pack. Small scraps of foil are worth saving for this.

FREEZING HINT

For slimmers, thicken casseroles at the end of cooking time, so you can remove a portion for them before thickening the rest.

49 Corn hot pot

You will need . . .

Cooking time
1¼–1½ hours

Oven setting
180°C, 350°F, Gas Mark 4

Storage time
4–6 months

Defrosting time
4 hours at room temperature and 40 minutes in the oven

1 tablespoon oil
4 large pork chops
1 large onion, sliced
2 tablespoons flour
300 ml/½ pint chicken stock
4 carrots, sliced
1 (326-g/11½-oz) can sweetcorn with peppers
salt and pepper
¼ teaspoon Tabasco or Worcestershire sauce
½ teaspoon paprika pepper
When serving:
watercress

Heat the oil and use to fry the chops until brown all over. Transfer them to an ovenproof casserole or foil container.

Add the onion to the fat in the pan and fry until golden brown. Stir in the flour and cook for 1 minute, then gradually add the stock. Bring to the boil, stirring constantly. Stir in the carrots, sweetcorn and liquid from the can and seasonings, and cook for 3 minutes.

Pour the sauce over the chops, cover and cook in a moderate oven for 1 hour. Cool.

To freeze: Cover dish with lid and secure with freezer tape or cover container with lid or foil. Seal and label.
To serve: Uncover to defrost then reheat in a moderate oven for 40 minutes. Garnish with watercress.
Serves 4

FREEZING HINT

The layer of fat and skin which one often requires to trim from pork chops can be turned into crackling in the oven and freezes well for about 1 month. It can quickly be crisped up in the oven and added to casseroles, soups or cooked vegetables.

50 Pork and prune hot pot

You will need . . .

Cooking time
about 1¾ hours

Oven setting
180°C, 350°F, Gas Mark 4

Storage time
4–6 months

Defrosting time
4–6 hours in the refrigerator and 35 minutes in the oven

4 pork sparerib chops
2 onions, sliced
salt and pepper
100 g/4 oz tenderised prunes
450 ml/¾ pint dry cider
2 tablespoons redcurrant jelly
2 tablespoons lemon juice
When serving:
150 ml/¼ pint soured cream
chopped parsley

Put the chops in an ovenproof casserole or foil container with the onion, seasoning and prunes.

Heat the cider with the redcurrant jelly and stir until the jelly has melted. Add the lemon juice and pour over the pork and prunes.

Cover and cook in a moderate oven for 1½ hours. Cool.

To freeze: Cover with lid and secure with freezer tape, or with foil. Seal and label.
To serve: Uncover to defrost then reheat in a moderate oven for 30 minutes. Stir the soured cream into the sauce, reserving a spoonful for garnish, and return to the oven for a further 5 minutes. Serve garnished with the spoonful of cream and chopped parsley.
Serves 4

FREEZING HINT

For a different flavour, or if you have no cider, substitute an equivalent amount of strained sweetened black tea.

51 Spicy apricot ham rolls

52 Bacon slipper stew

You will need . . .

Cooking time
about 20 minutes

Oven setting
200°C, 400°F, Gas Mark 6

Storage time
3–4 months

Defrosting time
2 hours at room temperature and 30–35 minutes in the oven

100 g/4 oz dried apricots, soaked overnight
25 g/1 oz butter
50 g/2 oz dry wholemeal breadcrumbs
1 teaspoon dry mustard
½ teaspoon ground ginger
pinch ground cloves
25 g/1 oz sugar
8 slices ham
100 g/4 oz brown sugar
4 tablespoons cider vinegar
5 whole cloves
2.5-cm/1-inch length cinnamon stick

Cook the apricots in water until tender. Drain and reserve 150 ml/¼ pint of the cooking liquid. Mince or chop the apricots. Melt the butter in a small saucepan, stir in the chopped apricots, breadcrumbs, mustard, ginger, ground cloves and 25 g/1 oz sugar.

Spread the apricot stuffing on to the ham slices, roll up and fasten each with a wooden cocktail stick. Place the ham rolls in a greased shallow foil container.

Simmer the apricot cooking liquid with the brown sugar, cider vinegar, cloves and cinnamon stick for 5 minutes. Strain over the ham rolls and cool.

To freeze: Cover with lid. Seal and label.
To serve: Defrost at room temperature, uncover and reheat in a moderately hot oven, basting frequently with the sauce. Serve garnished with sprigs of watercress.
Serves 4

You will need . . .

Cooking time
1¼–1½ hours

Storage time
3–4 months

Defrosting time
4 hours at room temperature then reheat in a saucepan

750 g/1½–1¾ lb slipper of bacon
40 g/1½ oz butter
1 large onion, chopped
1 large parsnip, diced
1 medium swede, diced
2 tablespoons flour
1½ teaspoons dry mustard
600 ml/1 pint chicken stock
2 tablespoons orange jelly marmalade
salt and pepper
100 g/4 oz frozen peas

Remove the rind from the bacon and cut the meat into 2.5-cm/1-inch cubes. Put them in a saucepan, cover with cold water, stir well and bring to the boil. Simmer for 5–10 minutes. Drain well.

Meanwhile, melt the butter in a saucepan and gently fry the onion, parsnip and swede for 5 minutes, until softened but not coloured. Stir in the flour and mustard and cook for 1 minute. Gradually add the stock and bring to the boil, stirring constantly. Cook for 2 minutes, add the marmalade and pepper to taste then stir in the bacon pieces.

Cover and simmer for 1 hour, or until the bacon is tender. Stir in the peas, adjust the seasoning and cool.

To freeze: Pack in a polythene or foil container. Seal and label.
To serve: Uncover to defrost then turn into a saucepan and reheat gently to boiling point. Simmer for 5 minutes and serve with baked potatoes, if liked.
Serves 4–5

FREEZING HINT

Make up and freeze stuffing mixtures before they are required. If used to stuff a bird or joint before freezing, the stuffing will shorten the storage time of the meat to 3 months only.

FREEZING HINT

To save time when preparing stews, freeze small mixed packs of unblanched root vegetables. Use them up fairly quickly, because unblanched vegetables do not always have a long freezer life.

53 Simmered Kofta balls

Beef, beer
54 and walnut casserole

You will need . . .

Cooking time
15–20 minutes

Storage time
3–4 months

Defrosting time
4 hours at room temperature
then reheat in a saucepan

450 g/1 lb finely minced beef
2 tablespoons ground rice
1 large onion, grated
1 clove garlic, crushed
½ teaspoon ground allspice
pinch ground cloves
salt and black pepper
1 tablespoon chopped parsley
50 g/2 oz seedless raisins
oil for frying
15 g/½ oz butter
1 tablespoon flour
450 ml/¾ pint tomato juice

Place the beef, rice, onion and garlic in a bowl. Sprinkle over the allspice, cloves, salt, pepper, parsley and raisins. Knead well together, with a wooden spoon or by hand.

Form the mixture into small balls, and shallow fry gently in hot oil for 10–15 minutes, turning frequently until brown all over. Drain well.

Meanwhile, melt the butter in a saucepan and stir in the flour. Cook for 1 minute then gradually add the tomato juice and bring to the boil, stirring all the time. Simmer for 3 minutes, season to taste and cool.

To freeze: Pack the meatballs and sauce together in a polythene container. Seal and label.
To serve: Uncover to defrost then turn into a saucepan and reheat gently to boiling point. Simmer for 5 minutes, garnish with parsley and serve with fluffy boiled rice.
Serves 4

You will need . . .

Cooking time
2½ hours

Storage time
4–6 months

Defrosting time
overnight in the refrigerator
then reheat in a saucepan

2 tablespoons oil
25 g/1 oz butter
1 onion, sliced
450 g/1 lb stewing steak, cubed
40 g/1½ oz seasoned flour
300 ml/½ pint brown ale
450 ml/¾ pint stock
50 g/2 oz walnut halves or pieces
salt and pepper
When serving:
chopped parsley

Heat the oil and butter in a saucepan and use to fry the onion for 5 minutes.

Dust the cubed meat with seasoned flour. Add to the onion and fry until the meat is brown on all sides. Stir in the remaining seasoned flour. Gradually add the brown ale and stock and bring to the boil, stirring constantly.

Cover and simmer for 2 hours, adding the walnuts for the last 30 minutes. Taste and adjust for seasoning. Cool.

To freeze: Pack in a polythene container. Seal and label.
To serve: Uncover to defrost then turn into a saucepan and reheat gently to boiling point, stirring carefully from time to time. Simmer for 5 minutes and sprinkle with chopped parsley.
Serves 4

FREEZING HINT

Leftover stock should be reduced until very strong, and used to fill as many sections of an ice cube tray as possible. The empty spaces can be filled next time you have a little stock to spare.

FREEZING HINT

Particularly if your family loves gravy, any surplus should be frozen in small containers to reheat and serve with meat meals which do not naturally produce juices to make gravy.

Kidneys
55 in redcurrant sauce

You will need . . .

450 g/1 lb ox kidney
25 g/1 oz butter
1 tablespoon vinegar
300 ml/½ pint dry ginger ale
1 tablespoon redcurrant jelly
25 g/1 oz sultanas
100 g/4 oz mushrooms, quartered
1 tablespoon gravy powder
salt and pepper
2 tablespoons single cream
When serving:
chopped parsley

Cooking time
about 55 minutes

Storage time
3–4 months

Defrosting
Reheat from frozen in boiling water

Skin and chop the kidney, removing the core. Melt the butter and fry the kidney until it changes colour, then add the vinegar and ginger ale. Bring to the boil, cover and simmer for 30 minutes.

Add the redcurrant jelly, sultanas and mushrooms and stir until the jelly has completely melted. Moisten the gravy powder with a little cold water and add to the pan. Bring to the boil, stirring all the time, until thickened and smooth. Simmer for 10 minutes. Taste and adjust for seasoning, stir in the cream and cool.

To freeze: Pack in a boiling bag. Seal and label.
To serve: Place the bag, still frozen, in a pan of boiling water. Bring back to the boil, simmer for 30–40 minutes. Garnish with chopped parsley and serve with French bread.
Serves 4

FREEZING HINT

Redcurrant, gooseberry and apple-mint jellies all store better in the freezer than in a cupboard. Refrigerate after opening and use up within one week.

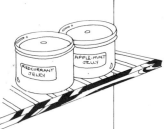

Liver and
56 green pepper casserole

You will need . . .

450 g/1 lb ox liver, sliced
milk
seasoned flour
2 green peppers
1 onion, sliced
1 (396-g/14-oz) can tomatoes
150 ml/¼ pint stock
1 tablespoon tomato purée
1 tablespoon sugar
1 teaspoon dried mixed herbs

Cooking time
1¼ hours

Oven setting
180°C, 350°F, Gas Mark 4

Storage time
3–4 months

Defrosting time
overnight in the refrigerator and 30 minutes in the oven

Soak the liver slices in milk for 2 hours. Drain and coat lightly in seasoned flour. Deseed and slice the green peppers. Arrange the liver in layers with the sliced onion and green pepper, in an ovenproof casserole or foil container.

Mix together the tomatoes and liquid from the can, the stock, tomato purée, sugar and herbs and pour over the liver and vegetables.

Cover and cook in a moderate oven for 1¼ hours. Cool.

To freeze: Cover casserole with lid and secure with freezer tape, or cover container with lid or foil. Seal and label.
To serve: Uncover to defrost then reheat in a moderate oven for 30 minutes.
Serves 4

FREEZING HINT

Many casserole dishes could be reheated in less time in a moderately hot oven than in a moderate one, especially if you have another dish to cook at the same time and can therefore economise on the oven heat.

57 Pigeons in red wine

You will need . . .

Cooking time
about 1¼ hours

Oven setting
180°C, 350°F, Gas Mark 4
190°C, 375°F, Gas Mark 5

Storage time
4–6 months

Defrosting time
overnight in the refrigerator
or 4–6 hours at room
temperature and 30 minutes
in the oven

50 g/2 oz butter
2 plump pigeons, split
4 small rashers streaky bacon, chopped
225 g/8 oz baby onions
100 g/4 oz baby carrots
100 g/4 oz button mushrooms
150 ml/¼ pint red wine
1 (439-g/15½-oz) can butter beans
4 peppercorns
1 bay leaf
salt and pepper

Melt the butter and fry the pigeon halves on all sides for 5 minutes. Transfer to an ovenproof casserole.

Use the fat remaining in the pan to fry the bacon gently until the fat runs. Add the onions, carrots and mushrooms and cook gently for 3–4 minutes. Pour in the wine and bring to the boil, stirring well. Add the sauce to the casserole with the liquid from the can of butter beans, the peppercorns and bay leaf. Sprinkle with salt, cover and cook in a moderate oven for 1 hour. Taste and adjust for seasoning, stir in the butter beans and cool.

To freeze: Cover with lid and seal with freezer tape or transfer to a foil container. Seal and label.
To serve: Uncover to defrost, then reheat in a moderately hot oven for 30 minutes.
Serves 4

FREEZING HINT

To tenderise pigeon, for party dishes, remove the breasts from the raw birds then boil the legs and carcases in water to make a stock. Add a little vinegar, oil and seasoning, then marinate the breasts in closed containers for 2 days before freezing.

58 Rabbit and orange stew

You will need . . .

Cooking time
1¾ hours

Storage time
4–6 months

Defrosting time
overnight in the refrigerator
then reheat in a saucepan

4 rabbit portions
150 ml/¼ pint fresh orange juice
pinch ground mixed spice
salt and pepper
1 small onion, sliced
2 tablespoons chopped parsley
seasoned flour
25 g/1 oz butter
2 tablespoons oil
450 ml/¾ pint chicken stock
When serving:
2 oranges
sprigs of watercress

Put the rabbit portions in a shallow dish with the orange juice, mixed spice, seasoning, onion and parsley. Cover and chill for at least 4 hours, to marinate.

Drain the rabbit joints on absorbent paper, reserving the marinade. Dust lightly in seasoned flour.

Heat the butter and oil in a large saucepan and use to brown the rabbit joints on all sides. Add the marinade and stock and bring to the boil, stirring. Cover and simmer for 1½ hours. Cool.

To freeze: Pack in a polythene container. Seal and label.
To serve: Uncover to defrost. Grate the zest from the oranges, then peel and divide them into segments. Turn the stew into a saucepan, add the orange zest and reheat gently to boiling point. Stir in the orange segments and simmer for a further 5 minutes. Garnish with sprigs of watercress and serve with floury boiled potatoes.
Serves 4

FREEZING HINT

When herbs are plentiful, freeze them in small bunches in polythene bags, or chopped with a little water in ice cube trays. Store the cubes in polythene bags and add them straight to stews, soups or casseroles.

Chicken meatball
59 and olive casserole

You will need . . .

Cooking time
about 1 hour

Oven setting
180°C, 350°F, Gas Mark 4

Storage time
4–6 months

Defrosting time
4–6 hours in the refrigerator
and 30–40 minutes in the
oven

350 g/12 oz boned raw chicken
1 onion, quartered
1 (99-g/3½-oz) packet sage and onion
  stuffing mix
2 egg yolks
salt and pepper
grated zest of 1 orange
2 tablespoons oil
1 onion, sliced
2 carrots, sliced
25 g/1 oz flour
750 ml/1¼ pints chicken stock
50 g/2 oz stuffed green olives
2 tablespoons chopped parsley

Mince the chicken with the onion. Make up the stuffing mix according to packet directions, using slightly less liquid. Combine with the egg yolks, minced chicken and onion, salt, pepper and orange zest. Form into 12 balls. Heat the oil and fry the onion and carrot for 5 minutes. Stir in the flour and cook for 1 minute. Gradually add the stock and bring to the boil, stirring. Lower the meatballs into the sauce and simmer for 45 minutes. Adjust the seasoning, add the olives and parsley and cool.

To freeze: Pack in a foil container and cover with lid or foil. Seal and label.
To serve: Uncover to defrost then reheat in a moderate oven for 30–40 minutes.
Serves 4–6
Note: If using the Slo Cooker (as illustrated) treble the quantities and refer to the instructions for cooking times.

FREEZING HINT

Small foil parcels of blanched frozen vegetables do not need to be turned into a saucepan to be cooked when the oven is in use; just pop the parcel into the oven for 20–25 minutes, according to the oven temperature.

Barbecued
60 chicken stew

You will need . . .

Cooking time
about 1 hour

Storage time
4–6 months

Defrosting time
overnight in the refrigerator
and then reheat in a
saucepan

225 g/8 oz frankfurter sausages
2 tablespoons oil
8 chicken wing tips
1 onion, grated
1 tablespoon curry powder
2 teaspoons Worcestershire sauce
1 tablespoon brown sugar
1 tablespoon French mustard
1 tablespoon tomato purée
450 ml/¾ pint chicken stock
salt and pepper

Slice the frankfurters diagonally into 2.5-cm/1-inch chunks.
  Heat the oil in a saucepan and use to fry the chicken gently with the onion and curry powder for 5 minutes. Add all the remaining ingredients and bring to the boil.
  Cover and simmer for 45 minutes. Cool.

To freeze: Pack in a foil container and cover with lid or foil. Seal and label.
To serve: Uncover to defrost then turn into a saucepan and reheat gently to boiling point, stirring carefully from time to time. Simmer for 5 minutes and serve with fluffy boiled rice.
Serves 4

FREEZING HINT

If a frozen casserole dish seems to taste over-spicy when defrosted, add diced peeled raw potato to the dish while reheating. This will absorb some of the spiciness and restore the balance of flavour.

Corn
61 and tuna casserole

You will need . . .

Cooking time
about 20 minutes

Storage time
2–3 months

Defrosting time
30 minutes in boiling water
from frozen or reheat from
frozen in a saucepan

50 g/ 2 oz butter
100 g/4 oz button mushrooms, sliced
25 g/1 oz flour
1 chicken stock cube
1 (198-g/7-oz) can tuna
450 ml/¾ pint milk
1 (340-g/12-oz) can sweetcorn
50 g/2 oz peeled prawns
salt and freshly ground black pepper

Melt the butter in a saucepan and fry the mushroom slices
until golden. Remove and drain well.

Stir the flour into the butter remaining in the pan.
Crumble in the stock cube and add the liquid from the can
of tuna. Gradually add the milk and bring to the boil,
stirring. Break up the tuna and add to the sauce.

Cover and simmer for 5 minutes. Stir in the sweetcorn
and liquid from the can, the fried mushrooms and the
prawns. Season to taste with salt and pepper and cool.

To freeze: Pack in a boiling bag or polythene-lined
carton. Seal and label.
To serve: Place the bag in a pan of boiling water, bring
back to the boil and simmer for 30 minutes, or turn the
frozen casserole into a saucepan and reheat gently to
boiling point. Serve with fried garlic croûtons (see recipe
16) and green peas, if liked.
Serves 4

FREEZING HINT

*Make casserole dishes without
seasoning, remove a portion to
purée or blend for a baby or an
invalid, then season the remainder.*

62 Cheesy fish bake

You will need . . .

Cooking time
about 30 minutes

Oven setting
180°C, 350°F, Gas Mark 4

Storage time
4–6 months

Defrosting time
35 minutes in the oven from
frozen

1 medium onion, chopped
1 (227-g/8-oz) can tomatoes
150 ml/¼ pint fish or chicken stock
salt and pepper
4 plaice fillets
4 tablespoons bottled tartare sauce
100 g/4 oz Edam cheese
2 tablespoons dried breadcrumbs
15 g/½ oz butter
When serving:
sprigs of watercress

Place the chopped onion in a saucepan with the tomatoes
and their juice and the stock. Bring to the boil and simmer
for about 10 minutes, until the onion is soft. Season to
taste with salt and pepper.

Meanwhile skin the plaice fillets and spread each with a
tablespoon of tartare sauce. Cut the cheese into 4 oblong
pieces. Wrap each fish fillet round a piece of cheese, with
the sauce inside, and secure with a wooden cocktail stick.
Arrange in a greased foil container or ovenproof dish.

Pour the tomato mixture round the fish rolls, sprinkle
the fish with the breadcrumbs and dot with the butter.
Bake in a moderate oven for 15–20 minutes. Cool.

To freeze: Cover with foil. Seal and label.
To serve: Place still frozen in a moderate oven for 30
minutes. Remove the covering and return to the oven for a
further 5 minutes. Serve garnished with watercress.
Serves 4

FREEZING HINT

*To prevent fish from dehydrating
in the frozen state, freeze until
solid, dip into iced water until a
thin coating of ice is formed, then
return to the freezer until the
coating of ice is solid. Repeat
until the ice is about 5 mm/¼ inch
thick, then pack in foil and seal.*

63 Spicy fish casserole

You will need . . .

Cooking time
about 1¼ hours

Oven setting
180°C, 350°F, Gas Mark 4

Storage time
4–6 months

Defrosting time
3 hours in the refrigerator
and 30 minutes in the oven

25 g/1 oz butter
40 g/1½ oz flour
150 ml/¼ pint milk
300 ml/½ pint fish or chicken stock
1 teaspoon paprika pepper
½ teaspoon Tabasco sauce
2 teaspoons Worcestershire sauce
2 tablespoons drained capers
grated zest of ½ lemon
450 g/1 lb coley
225 g/8 oz tomatoes, sliced
2 sticks celery, chopped

Melt the butter in a pan and stir in the flour. Cook for 1 minute. Gradually add the milk and stock and bring to the boil, stirring constantly. Add the paprika, Tabasco, Worcestershire sauce, capers and lemon zest.

Divide the coley into 4 pieces. Place in a shallow ovenproof dish or foil container and top with the tomatoes and celery.

Pour over the spicy sauce and cook in a moderate oven for 1 hour. Cool.

To freeze: Cover dish with lid and secure with freezer tape, or cover container with lid or foil. Seal and label.
To serve: Uncover to defrost, then reheat in a moderate oven for 30 minutes.
Serves 4

FREEZING HINT

Over-wrap any foods which might have a strong smell. It is much easier to take this precaution than to remove a clinging smell from your freezer cabinet.

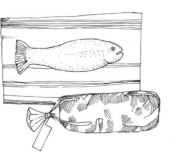

Haddock 64 and cider hot pot

You will need . . .

Cooking time
20–30 minutes

Oven setting
160°C, 325°F, Gas Mark 3

Storage time
4–6 months

Defrosting time
30 minutes in the oven from frozen

675 g/1½ lb fresh haddock
salt and pepper
225 g/8 oz tomatoes
2 medium onions, chopped
150 ml/¼ pint dry cider
pinch dried mixed herbs
3 tablespoons soft white breadcrumbs
50 g/2 oz Gouda cheese, grated
When serving:
lemon slice
parsley

Skin the haddock, divide into 4 portions and place these in a greased foil container or ovenproof dish. Sprinkle with salt and pepper.

Skin and slice the tomatoes and arrange over the fish with the chopped onion. Pour on the cider and sprinkle over the herbs and more seasoning.

Cover and cook in a moderate oven for 20–30 minutes, until the fish is cooked. Remove the lid, sprinkle with the breadcrumbs and cheese and cool.

To freeze: Cover with foil. Seal and label.
To serve: Place still covered and frozen in a moderate oven for 20 minutes, remove the covering and return to the oven for a further 10 minutes. Serve garnished with a twist of lemon and sprig of parsley.
Serves 4

FREEZING HINT

Try combining gooseberries with herb and breadcrumb stuffings for oily fish such as mackerel, or making them into jelly to serve with meat and game as an alternative to redcurrant jelly.

Vegetarian
65 bean hot pot

You will need . . .

Cooking time
2½ hours

Oven setting
150°C, 300°F, Gas Mark 2
200°C, 400°F, Gas Mark 6

Storage time
4–6 months

Defrosting time
6 hours in the refrigerator
and 30 minutes in the oven

175 g/6 oz dried kidney beans
2 large leeks
2 large carrots, sliced
225 g/8 oz potatoes, sliced
1 onion, chopped
salt and pepper
175 g/6 oz cheese, grated
1 clove garlic, crushed
750 ml/1¼ pints vegetable stock
When serving:
slices of French bread
grated cheese
chopped parsley

Soak the kidney beans in cold water overnight, then drain. Cut the leeks into rings and rinse well in a colander under running water.

Arrange the beans, leeks, carrots, potato and onion in an ovenproof dish or foil container, sprinkling with the seasoning and grated cheese. Stir the crushed garlic into the stock and pour over the vegetable mixture.

Cover and cook in a cool oven for 2½ hours. Cool.

To freeze: Secure lid with freezer tape, or cover container with lid or foil. Seal and label.
To serve: Uncover to defrost, then top with an overlapping ring of French bread slices, generously sprinkled with cheese. Reheat and crisp the top in a moderately hot oven for 30 minutes. Scatter chopped parsley to garnish.
Serves 4

FREEZING HINT

For non-vegetarians, reduce the amount of cheese by half and substitute diced salami sausage.

Gouda
66 and potato casserole

You will need . . .

Cooking time
35 minutes

Oven setting
190°C, 375°F, Gas Mark 5

Storage time
4–6 months

Defrosting time
40–45 minutes in the oven
from frozen

675 g/1½ lb potatoes, sliced
225 g/8 oz bacon
175 g/6 oz Gouda cheese, grated
1 large onion, chopped
1 tablespoon chopped parsley
salt and pepper
25 g/1 oz flour
150 ml/¼ pint vegetable or chicken stock
When serving:
chopped parsley

Boil the potato slices in salted water for 5 minutes. Drain well. Derind and chop the bacon.

Reserve one third of the cheese and layer the rest in a greased foil container or casserole dish with the potato, bacon, onion and parsley. Sprinkle with salt and pepper. Blend together the flour and the stock until smooth, pour over the casserole ingredients and sprinkle with the remaining cheese.

Cook in a moderately hot oven for 30 minutes. Cool.

To freeze: Cover with lid or foil, securing casserole lid with freezer tape. Seal and label.
To serve: Uncover and place still frozen in a moderately hot oven for 40–45 minutes. Serve garnished with chopped parsley.
Serves 4

FREEZING HINT

Wiener Schnitzel – pork fillet costs less than veal. Slice fairly thick then bat out thinly. Coat with egg and breadcrumbs, ready for frying from frozen. Or spread with savoury stuffing, roll up and tie with thread, all ready to make savoury 'birds'.

67 Curried cauliflower and carrots

You will need . . .

1 small cauliflower
300 ml/10 fl oz natural yogurt
1 small onion, grated
1 clove garlic, crushed
½ teaspoon ground ginger
450 g/1 lb carrots, sliced
50 g/2 oz butter
1 large onion, chopped
1 tablespoon curry powder
150 ml/¼ pint hot water
¼ teaspoon salt
When serving:
½ teaspoon ground coriander

Cooking time
about 25 minutes

Storage time
3–4 months

Defrosting time
25 minutes in boiling water
from frozen

Trim and divide the cauliflower into florets. Mix the yogurt, grated onion, garlic and ginger in a bowl. Add the cauliflower florets and carrot slices and coat well. Cover and leave for 2 hours, to marinate.

Melt the butter in a large pan and brown the chopped onion. Stir in the curry powder and cook for 1 minute. Add the vegetables and marinade, the hot water and the salt.

Bring to the boil, stirring, then simmer for 10–15 minutes, or until the vegetables are just tender but still slightly crunchy. Cool.

To freeze: Pack in a boiling bag. Seal and label.
To serve: Place the bag in a pan of boiling water, return to the boil and simmer for 25 minutes. Serve sprinkled with coriander.
Serves 4

FREEZING HINT

Vegetables with a long cropping season, such as runner beans, are best picked every few days. Cook larger specimens for immediate eating in the pan you use to blanch smaller ones for freezing.

68 Aubergine potato bake

You will need . . .

3 large aubergines, sliced
salt and black pepper
1 large onion, chopped
oil for frying
1 (396-g/14-oz) can tomatoes
1 teaspoon dried oregano
100 g/4 oz garlic sausage, sliced
450 g/1 lb potatoes, sliced
2 tomatoes, sliced
1 tablespoon dry breadcrumbs
2 tablespoons grated Parmesan cheese

Cooking time
about 45 minutes

Oven setting
190°C, 375°F, Gas Mark 5

Storage time
3–4 months

Defrosting time
4 hours at room temperature
and 30 minutes in the oven

Sprinkle the aubergine slices with salt, allow to stand for 30 minutes, then rinse, drain and pat dry.

Meanwhile, fry the onion in 2 tablespoons oil in a large frying pan until soft. Remove and place in a saucepan with the tomatoes, oregano and seasoning to taste. Cover and simmer for 20 minutes, then stir in the garlic sausage.

Fry the aubergine and potato slices in the frying pan, adding more oil as required, until tender. Fill a greased foil container or casserole dish with alternate layers of potato aubergine mixture and tomato sauce, ending with the potato aubergine mixture. Cover with the tomato slices and sprinkle with the breadcrumbs and cheese. Cool.

To freeze: Cover with lid or foil, securing casserole lid with freezer tape. Seal and label.
To serve: Uncover to defrost, then reheat in a moderately hot oven for 30 minutes.
Serves 4

FREEZING HINT

Freeze bags of grated leftover cheese with breadcrumbs to make quick toppings for savoury dishes. Crumble the pack between your hands while still frozen.

Poultry cook-ins

Clever cooks are turning more and more to poultry for a greater variety of main meal dishes. Turkey is almost as popular as chicken and many of the dishes here can be adapted to use either meat. The recipes are as tempting as their titles, yet amazingly simple to produce; try Spiced garlic chicken or Thai festival duck.

There are recipes using frozen chickens and chicken portions, as well as ideas for turning already cooked meat into tasty dishes. It is perfectly safe to freeze cooked chicken dishes where a frozen bird has originally been used, provided the dish is cooked and frozen in the shortest possible time.

69 Gingered drumsticks

(illustrated on frontispiece)

You will need . . .

Cooking time
25–35 minutes

Oven setting
190°C, 375°F, Gas Mark 5

Storage time
4–6 months

Defrosting time
4 hours at room temperature and 25 minutes in the oven

8 chicken drumsticks
seasoned flour
oil for frying
For the sauce:
4 pieces preserved ginger
2 tablespoons ginger syrup, from the jar
2 tablespoons lemon juice
4 tablespoons dry sherry
25 g/1 oz butter
When serving:
mustard and cress

Remove the skin from the drumsticks and coat them in seasoned flour. Heat the oil and fry the drumsticks gently for about 15–20 minutes, until tender and golden brown all over. Drain off all the oil.

Finely chop the ginger and place in a saucepan with the ginger syrup, lemon juice, sherry and butter. Bring to the boil, stirring, and pour over the chicken. Cover and simmer gently for a further 10–15 minutes. Cool.

To freeze: Pack in a foil container. Seal and label.
To serve: Uncover to defrost then reheat in a moderately hot oven for 25 minutes. Garnish with mustard and cress.
Serves 4

Chicken
70 with pineapple sauce

You will need . . .

Cooking time
about 25 minutes

Oven setting
190°C, 375°F, Gas Mark 5

Storage time
4–6 months

Defrosting time
4 hours at room temperature and 25 minutes in the oven

4 chicken portions
oil for frying
½ cucumber
4 sticks celery
2 tomatoes, peeled
1 (227-g/8-oz) can pineapple cubes
2 tablespoons soy sauce
1 tablespoon wine vinegar
2 teaspoons Worcestershire sauce
1 tablespoon cornflour
salt and pepper
1 tablespoon chopped parsley

Fry the chicken portions in hot oil for about 20 minutes, until golden brown all over and cooked through. Drain.

Meanwhile, cut the cucumber, celery and deseeded tomatoes into narrow strips. Drain the pineapple cubes and make the syrup up to 600 ml/1 pint with water.

Blend together the soy sauce, vinegar, Worcestershire sauce and cornflour in a saucepan. Add the pineapple liquid and stir until smooth. Bring to the boil, stirring all the time. Add the cucumber, celery, tomato and pineapple cubes. Stir well and season to taste. Cook for 15 minutes. Stir in the parsley and cool.

To freeze: Pack the chicken portions in a polythene container and spoon over the sauce. Seal and label.
To serve: Uncover to defrost, transfer to a casserole dish then reheat in a moderately hot oven for 25 minutes.
Serves 4

FREEZING HINT

Chicken fat skimmed from the top of chicken stock is ideal for making chicken-flavoured croûtons to freeze. Pack by usual method.

FREEZING HINT

To test whether fried chicken portions are fully cooked, pierce with a fine skewer. The juices should be colourless; if still pink the chicken is not quite ready.

Peanut-crusted 71 chicken portions

You will need . . .

Cooking time
about 15 minutes

Storage time
4–6 months

Defrosting time
4 hours at room temperature
and 10–15 minutes in hot
oil for the chicken
15 minutes in boiling water
from frozen for the sauce

2 tablespoons corn oil
2 tablespoons wine vinegar
few drops Tabasco
2 tablespoons peanut butter
2 cloves garlic, crushed
salt and pepper
8 chicken thigh portions, skinned
flour for coating
2 eggs, beaten
50 g/2 oz toasted breadcrumbs
50 g/2 oz salted peanuts, chopped
oil for frying
2 teaspoons cornflour
about 4 tablespoons pineapple juice

Whisk the first six ingredients together, pour over the chicken portions and chill for 2 hours, to marinate. Drain the portions and pat dry. Coat in flour then in beaten egg then in the mixed breadcrumbs and peanuts. Shallow fry in hot oil for 5–10 minutes on each side. Cool.

Mix the cornflour with the pineapple juice. Bring to the boil with the marinade, stirring. Cook for 2 minutes and cool.

To freeze: Pack the portions in a polythene container with dividers and the sauce in a boiling bag. Seal and label.
To serve: Unpack the portions to defrost then refry in hot oil for 10–15 minutes. Place the bag of sauce in a pan of boiling water, boil and simmer for 15 minutes. Garnish the chicken with watercress to serve.
Serves 4

FREEZING HINT

Cook corn cobs from frozen in cold water otherwise the cob will remain frozen. Bring to the boil and simmer for about 5 minutes, according to the size of the cob.

Cheese- 72 stuffed chicken Kiev

You will need . . .

Storage time
4–6 months

Defrosting time
4 hours at room temperature
and 10 minutes in hot oil

4 small chicken breasts, boned and
skinned
175 g/6 oz Gouda cheese, grated
2 tablespoons chopped parsley
pinch pepper
For the coating:
seasoned flour
1 egg, beaten
toasted breadcrumbs
When serving:
oil for frying
lemon wedges
parsley

Place the chicken breasts between 2 sheets of foil or polythene and bat out thinly, taking care not to split the meat.

Combine the grated cheese, parsley and pepper and divide between the four chicken portions. Roll them up, like envelopes, and coat carefully in seasoned flour. Add 2 tablespoons water to the beaten egg and place the breadcrumbs in a shallow dish.

Coat the chicken envelopes in the egg mixture and roll in the breadcrumbs, taking care to seal completely.

To freeze: Pack in a rigid container with dividers. Seal and label.
To serve: Unpack to defrost then deep fry in hot oil for 10 minutes, until golden brown all over. Drain on kitchen paper and serve with lemon wedges and parsley.
Serves 4

FREEZING HINT

If you have no time to make stock from a chicken or turkey carcase, freeze it in a polythene bag until hard, wrap the bag in an old cloth, hammer flat with a rolling pin, then rebag the pieces until you decide to make stock.

73 Devilled chicken

You will need . . .

Cooking time
45 minutes

Oven setting
200°C, 400°F, Gas Mark 6

Storage time
4–6 months

Defrosting time
4 hours at room temperature
and 30 minutes in the oven

4 chicken portions
3 tablespoons oil
1 large mild onion, chopped
1 (340-g/12-oz) can sweetcorn
1 teaspoon Worcestershire sauce
1 tablespoon 'fruity' table sauce
1 tablespoon tomato ketchup
1 teaspoon prepared mustard
1 teaspoon Tabasco sauce
2 tablespoons vinegar
1 gherkin, chopped
1 tablespoon drained capers
salt and pepper

Brush the chicken portions with oil and place skin-side-down in a foil container or roasting pan. Bake in a moderately hot oven for 15 minutes then turn over and cook for a further 30 minutes.

Meanwhile, heat the remaining oil and gently cook the onion until soft. Add the remaining ingredients and bring to the boil, stirring constantly.

Adjust the seasoning, pour the sauce over the chicken and cool.

To freeze: Cover with lid or foil. Seal and label.
To serve: Uncover to defrost then reheat in a moderately hot oven for 30 minutes, basting the chicken twice with the sauce.
Serves 4

FREEZING HINT

Frozen whole tomatoes can be cut in half with a serrated knife and grilled or fried while semi-frozen. If completely defrosted they tend to lose their shape and texture.

74 Polish paprika chicken

You will need . . .

Cooking time
about 45 minutes

Oven setting
180°C, 350°F, Gas Mark 4
190°C, 375°F, Gas Mark 5

Storage time
4–6 months

Defrosting time
4 hours at room temperature
and 35 minutes in the oven

1 clove garlic, finely crushed
¼ teaspoon dried basil
pinch ground cloves
1 tablespoon mild paprika pepper
¼ teaspoon ground mace
40 g/1½ oz seasoned flour
4 chicken portions
1 tablespoon oil
25 g/1 oz butter
1 (70-g/2¾-oz) can red pimento
4 tablespoons dry sherry
1 tablespoon tomato purée
1 teaspoon sugar
When serving:
1 tablespoon chopped parsley
150 ml/¼ pint soured cream

Add the garlic, herbs and spices to the seasoned flour. Use to coat the chicken portions. Heat the oil and butter in a flameproof casserole and brown the chicken on all sides. Add the finely chopped pimento. Combine the liquid from the can with the sherry, tomato purée and sugar and pour over the chicken. Cover and cook in a moderate oven for 30 minutes, until tender. Cool.

To freeze: Pack in a foil container. Seal and label.
To serve: Uncover to defrost, then reheat in a moderately hot oven for 25 minutes. Mix the parsley with the soured cream, spoon over the chicken and return to the oven for a further 10 minutes.
Serves 4

FREEZING HINT

Frozen whole tomatoes are ideal for use in cooked dishes. To remove the skin, hold the frozen tomato under running cold water and the skin will slip off easily.

75 Spiced garlic chicken

You will need . . .

Cooking time
about 40 minutes

Oven setting
200°C, 400°F, Gas Mark 6

Storage time
3–4 months

Defrosting time
4 hours at room temperature
and 25 minutes in the oven

4 chicken portions
2 cloves garlic, crushed
½ teaspoon ground ginger
1 teaspoon ground turmeric
1 tablespoon oil
salt and pepper
1 green pepper
1 medium onion, chopped
½ teaspoon ground bay leaves
25 g/1 oz butter
150 ml/5 fl oz natural yogurt

Slash the chicken portions on both sides in several places. Mix the crushed garlic, ginger and turmeric with the oil and season well with salt and pepper. Spread over the chicken portions, pressing well into the slashes. Arrange in a foil container or ovenproof dish and allow to stand for 20 minutes. Bake in a moderately hot oven for 20 minutes.

Meanwhile, deseed and chop the green pepper and mix with the onion and bay leaves. Melt the butter and cook this mixture gently until soft. Remove from the heat, season with salt and stir in the yogurt. Pour over the chicken portions, cover lightly with foil and return to the oven for a further 20 minutes. Cool.

To freeze: Cover with lid or foil. Seal and label.
To serve: Uncover to defrost, then reheat in a moderately hot oven for 25 minutes. Serve with a cucumber and mint salad.
Serves 4

FREEZING HINT
To make a cucumber and mint salad, peel and thinly slice a small cucumber, spread out the slices on a board and sprinkle with salt. Stand for 20 minutes then rinse, drain, pat dry and serve sprinkled with chopped fresh mint leaves.

76 Sunshine chicken

You will need . . .

Cooking time
about 1½ hours

Oven setting
190°C, 375°F, Gas Mark 5

Storage time
4–6 months

Defrosting time
4 hours at room temperature
and 30 minutes in the oven

2 tablespoons oil
4 chicken portions
1 large onion, sliced
2 rashers bacon, chopped
50 g/2 oz mushrooms, sliced
finely grated zest and juice of 1 orange
1 (326-g/11½-oz) can sweetcorn with
    peppers
salt and pepper

Heat the oil and use to brown the chicken portions on all sides. Remove and drain well.

Add the onion and bacon to the pan and fry gently until golden brown. Add the mushrooms and fry for a further 2 minutes. Stir in the orange zest and juice and the sweetcorn and liquid from the can. Season well with salt and pepper and bring to the boil.

Spoon the corn mixture into a foil container or ovenproof dish and place the chicken portions on top. Cover with foil or lid and cook in a moderately hot oven for about 1 hour, until the chicken is tender. Cool.

To freeze: Cover with fresh foil or seal lid of dish with freezer tape. Seal and label.
To serve: Defrost while still sealed in the pack, then reheat in a moderately hot oven for 30 minutes. Serve garnished with orange slices and sprigs of parsley.
Serves 4

FREEZING HINT
Boiling fowls are often sold cheaply at freezer centres. If you have a pressure cooker, an average bird takes about 40 minutes to cook and costs far less in fuel than a roaster of the same weight would do in the oven.

77 Curried turkey

You will need . . .

Cooking time
2 hours

Storage time
4–6 months

Defrosting time
25 minutes in boiling water
from frozen

100 g/4 oz butter (or ghee)
450 g/1 lb onions, sliced
450 g/1 lb cooked turkey, diced
1½ teaspoons ground turmeric
2 teaspoons ground coriander
¾ teaspoon ground red chilli powder
1 teaspoon garam masala
½ teaspoon ground ginger
4 tablespoons tomato purée
1 (396-g/14-oz) can tomatoes
4 bay leaves
7.5-cm/3-inch piece cinnamon stick
6 cardamom seeds
6 cloves
salt

Melt the butter and use to fry the onion until soft. Add the meat and mix thoroughly.

Meanwhile, combine the turmeric, coriander, chilli, garam masala and ginger and sprinkle over the turkey mixture. Stir until blended. Add the remaining ingredients and mix well.

Cook over gentle heat for about 1¾ hours, adding a little water if the mixture gets too dry. Add salt to taste and cool. Remove the cinnamon stick.

To freeze: Pack in a boiling bag. Seal and label.
To serve: Place the bag, still frozen, in a pan of boiling water, return to the boil and simmer for 25 minutes. Serve with poppodums and cold side dishes.
Serves 4

FREEZING HINT

Side dishes for this curry include sliced cucumber in natural yogurt, orange segments with coconut, mango chutney, chopped tomatoes with green peppers and banana slices in lemon juice.

Turkey 78 with red dawn sauce

You will need . . .

Cooking time
10–15 minutes

Storage time
4–6 months

Defrosting time
25 minutes in boiling water
from frozen

2 teaspoons oil
10 tablespoons water
2 tablespoons vinegar
1½ teaspoons brown sugar
salt
2 teaspoons cornflour
450 g/1 lb cooked turkey, diced
2 teaspoons tomato purée
2 teaspoons soy sauce
175 g/6 oz carrot, grated
When serving:
sprig of parsley

Heat the oil and half the water, then carefully add the vinegar, the sugar and salt to taste. Bring to the boil.

Mix the cornflour with the rest of the water and blend into the sauce. Bring back to the boil, stirring constantly, and cook for 2–3 minutes.

Add the cooked turkey, tomato purée, soy sauce and grated carrot and reheat carefully to boiling point. Simmer for 5 minutes. Cool.

To freeze: Pack in a boiling bag. Seal and label.
To serve: Place the bag, still frozen, in a pan of boiling water, return to the boil and simmer for 25 minutes. Garnish with parsley and serve with fluffy boiled rice.
Serves 4

FREEZING HINT

Grapes frozen without added sugar, by the dry pack method, make a useful garnish to serve with white fish, a mild chicken curry or a rechauffé of cooked turkey in a savoury sauce.

79 Sweet-sour seconds
Duck
80 in black cherry sauce

79 Sweet-sour seconds

You will need . . .

400 g/14 oz cooked chicken or turkey
5 tablespoons flour
1 egg
1 tablespoon grated onion
3 tablespoons milk
oil for frying
For the sauce:
6 tablespoons water
2 tablespoons vinegar
2 tablespoons tomato ketchup
1 tablespoon soft brown sugar
1 tablespoon soy sauce
1 (225-g/8-oz) jar cranberry sauce
2 teaspoons cornflour
When serving:
oil for frying

Cooking time
about 15 minutes

Storage time
4–6 months

Defrosting time
Refry chicken from frozen in hot oil for 2 minutes
Reheat sauce from frozen in a saucepan

Cut the chicken or turkey into cubes. Beat the flour, egg and onion with the milk to form a thick batter. Coat the cubes in batter and fry in deep hot oil for 3 minutes, until crisp and golden. Drain on kitchen paper and cool.

Meanwhile, place the water in a pan with the vinegar, tomato ketchup, sugar and soy sauce. Sieve the cranberry sauce, stir in and bring to the boil. Moisten the cornflour with a little cold water, add to the pan and cook, stirring, until the sauce is thickened. Simmer for 2–3 minutes. Cool.

To freeze: Pack the chicken pieces in a rigid container and the sauce in a polythene container. Seal and label.
To serve: Refry chicken from frozen in deep hot oil for 2 minutes. Reheat sauce to boiling point in a saucepan. Serve with fluffy boiled rice.
Serves 4

80 Duck in black cherry sauce

You will need . . .

25 g/1 oz duck fat
2 small onions, grated
300 ml/½ pint duck or chicken stock
1 bay leaf
pinch ground cloves
salt and pepper
1 (425-g/15-oz) can black cherries
2 tablespoons cornflour
2 tablespoons port
450 g/1 lb boned cooked duck, sliced
When serving:
croûtons fried in duck fat
watercress

Cooking time
about 10 minutes

Storage time
4–6 months

Defrosting time
25 minutes in boiling water from frozen

Melt the fat and fry the onion gently until pale golden. Add the stock, bay leaf, cloves and seasoning. Stir well.

Drain the cherries and use 150 ml/¼ pint of the cherry syrup to moisten the cornflour. Add to the sauce and bring to the boil, stirring constantly. Cook gently for 2–3 minutes, until the sauce thickens. Remove the bay leaf and stir in the port. Add the cherries and duck meat to the sauce. Cool.

To freeze: Pack in a boiling bag. Seal and label.
To serve: Place the frozen bag in a saucepan of boiling water, bring back to the boil and simmer for 25 minutes. (If packed in a polythene container, defrost before reheating in a saucepan.) Garnish with crisp fried bread croûtons and watercress, and serve with a tomato and cucumber salad.
Serves 4

FREEZING HINT

If sauces are thin when reheated after freezing, sprinkle in 1 teaspoon gelatine to each 300 ml/½ pint of liquid and stir until completely dissolved. The sauce will thicken slightly when transferred to a serving jug.

FREEZING HINT

There is always a surplus of delicious fat from a roast duck. A good way to use this up is to fry bread croûtons in it. Cool well and freeze for short storage in small polythene containers.

Turkey fries
81 with Chinese vegetables

You will need . . .

Cooking time
about 6 minutes

Storage time
4–6 months

Defrosting time
20 minutes in a pan of boiling water for the sauce and 5–10 minutes in hot oil for the fries

1 green pepper
1 leek
oil for frying
100 g/4 oz bamboo shoots, sliced
100 g/4 oz fresh bean sprouts
225 g/8 oz cauliflower florets
For the sauce:
2 teaspoons cornflour
4 tablespoons water
2 tablespoons vinegar
25 g/1 oz sugar
1 tablespoon tomato ketchup
When serving:
1 (500-g/18-oz) pack turkey fries
oil for frying

Deseed and slice the green pepper. Trim and thinly slice the leek and rinse in a colander. Drain well.

Heat a little oil in a pan, add all the vegetables and cook briskly for 3 minutes, stirring continually. Drain off the oil.

Blend together the ingredients for the sauce, pour over the vegetables and bring to the boil, stirring all the time until the sauce thickens. Cool.

To freeze: Pack in a boiling bag. Seal and label.
To serve: Place the bag of sauce, still frozen, in a pan of boiling water and simmer for 20 minutes. Meanwhile, cook the turkey fries according to the instructions on the pack. Serve with soft egg noodles and the vegetable sauce.
Serves 4–6

FREEZING HINT

If you need to open a large can of water chestnuts or bamboo shoots for Chinese style cooking, any remaining will freeze perfectly re-packed in freezer containers.

Turkish chicken
82 with cardamom seeds

You will need . . .

Cooking time
20–30 minutes

4 frozen chicken portions
25 g/1 oz butter
1 teaspoon oil
1 tablespoon cardamom seeds or
    50 g/2 oz pine nuts
For the marinade:
150 ml/$\frac{1}{4}$ pint soured cream
1 tablespoon lemon juice
1 clove garlic, crushed
$\frac{1}{2}$ teaspoon ground cumin
$\frac{1}{2}$ teaspoon ground coriander
$\frac{1}{4}$ teaspoon freshly ground black pepper
1 teaspoon salt
When serving:
watercress

Place the chicken portions in a shallow dish. Combine all the ingredients for the marinade and pour over the chicken. Cover the dish and allow to stand overnight until the chicken is fully defrosted.

Lift out the chicken portions and place on a grid. Cook under a moderately hot grill for 20–30 minutes, according to the thickness of the portions. Turn the chicken pieces frequently and baste with the marinade.

Meanwhile, heat the butter and oil and use to fry the cardamom seeds or pine nuts. Scatter over the chicken portions, garnish with watercress and serve on a bed of saffron rice.
Serves 4

FREEZING HINT

If a frozen chicken takes longer to defrost than expected, shorten the roasting time by inserting a metal object, such as a large stainless steel spoon, inside the body cavity before placing the bird in the oven.

Chicken croquettes
83 with almonds

84 Vineyard chicken

You will need . . .

2 frozen chicken wing portions, defrosted
300 ml/½ pint chicken stock
40 g/1½ oz flaked almonds
50 g/2 oz butter
1 tablespoon flour
4 tablespoons milk
2 eggs
¼ teaspoon ground mace
salt and pepper
seasoned flour
toasted breadcrumbs
oil for frying
50 g/2 oz whole almonds, blanched

Cooking time
1–1¼ hours

Place the defrosted chicken portions in a saucepan with the stock. Cover and cook gently for 40 minutes, until tender. Cool in the stock. Remove the chicken, reserving the stock. Strip all the flesh and mince with the flaked almonds. Melt 15 g/½ oz of the butter in a saucepan and stir in the flour. Gradually stir in the milk and 3–4 tablespoons of the stock, to make a thick sauce. Blend in 1 egg yolk, the mace and seasoning to taste. Add the minced chicken and almonds and mix well. Chill.

Shape into 12 croquettes. Coat in seasoned flour, then in the beaten egg and egg white, and finally toss in the breadcrumbs. Fry the croquettes, 4 at a time, in deep hot oil for about 5 minutes, until crisp and golden brown. Drain well. Scatter over the almonds, fried in the remaining butter, and serve with a mixed salad.
Serves 4

You will need . . .

4 frozen chicken portions
150 ml/¼ pint dry white wine
50 g/2 oz butter
1 tablespoon oil
100 g/4 oz baby onions
salt and pepper
100 g/4 oz button mushrooms, halved
225 g/8 oz seedless white grapes
225 g/8 oz egg noodles
2 tablespoons chopped mixed herbs
2 teaspoons cornflour

Cooking time
about 40 minutes

Place the chicken portions in a shallow dish. Pour over the wine and allow to defrost overnight. Drain and pat dry on kitchen paper. Reserve the wine marinade.

Heat half the butter and the oil together and fry the onions until just tender but not browned. Add the chicken portions, sprinkle with salt and pepper and fry gently for 20 minutes, turning several times. Pour over the wine marinade, add the mushrooms and grapes and cook gently for 10 minutes.

Meanwhile, cook the noodles in plenty of salted boiling water, drain and toss with the remaining butter and the herbs. Remove the chicken portions from the sauce and keep hot. Moisten the cornflour with a little cold water, add to the sauce and bring to the boil, stirring constantly. Cook gently for 2 minutes until smooth and thickened. Serve the chicken portions on a bed of herbed noodles and spoon over the sauce.
Serves 4

FREEZING HINT

To freeze the croquettes, fry for 4 minutes only until pale golden. Re-fry from frozen or bake in a hot oven for 20 minutes.

FREEZING HINT

When seedless grapes are in season, freeze small quantities in syrup to add interest to fruit salads. Just strip them from the stalks and pack whole – there is no need to halve them.

Creamed
85 mushroom chicken

You will need . . .

Cooking time
about 1¾ hours

Oven setting
180°C, 350°F, Gas Mark 4

1 (1.5-kg/3½-lb) frozen roasting
   chicken, defrosted
25 g/1 oz flour
2 tablespoons oil
25 g/1 oz butter
50 g/2 oz flaked almonds
225 g/8 oz button mushrooms, sliced
150 ml/¼ pint chicken stock
salt and pepper
150 ml/¼ pint soured cream
When serving:
parsley

Sprinkle the chicken with the flour. Heat the oil and butter in a large saucepan and use to brown the chicken quickly all over. Lift out and place in an ovenproof casserole.

Use the fat remaining in the saucepan to fry the almonds and mushrooms until golden brown. Transfer to the casserole with the chicken stock and season to taste.

Cover and cook in a moderate oven for 1½ hours, or until the chicken is tender. Thirty minutes before serving, remove the lid and pour over the soured cream, mixing it well with the juices in the casserole. Baste the bird thoroughly with the mixture and return to the oven. Serve garnished with parsley.
Serves 4–6

FREEZING HINT

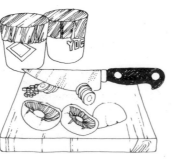

When preparing mushrooms, remove the stalks. Chop these very finely, season and sauté quickly in butter to make a concentrated mushroom paste. Pack in small containers, yogurt or cream cartons, and add to soups, stews, sauces and stuffings.

86 Herbed chicken in cider

You will need . . .

Cooking time
about 1½ hours

Oven setting
200°C, 400°F, Gas Mark 6

50 g/2 oz butter
2 tablespoons chopped mixed
   herbs (thyme, parsley, tarragon,
   marjoram, mint, oregano — as
   available)
1 clove garlic, crushed
salt and freshly ground black pepper
1 (1.5-kg/3½-lb) frozen roasting
   chicken, defrosted
300 ml/½ pint dry cider
1 tablespoon flour
4 tablespoons single cream

Cream together the butter and fresh herbs. Blend in the crushed garlic and season well with salt and pepper. Spread half the herb butter over the chicken and place the rest inside the body cavity.

Lay the chicken on its side on a grid in a roasting pan. Pour in the cider, roast in a moderately hot oven for 25 minutes. Turn the chicken on to the other side, baste and roast for a further 25 minutes. Turn the chicken, breast upwards, baste again and roast for a further 25 minutes.

Remove the chicken to a warm serving dish. Take the grid from the pan, skim off excess fat from the juices and combine this with the flour. Stir until smooth, return to the roasting pan and place over moderate heat, stirring all the time until the sauce is thickened and smooth. Taste and adjust for seasoning then stir in the cream and reheat without boiling. Spoon around the chicken to serve and garnish with watercress.
Serves 4–6

FREEZING HINT

Make giblet stock while the chicken is roasting and reserve it. Freeze, sliced leftover chicken in the stock to keep it moist.

Moroccan 87 jellied chicken

You will need . . .

1 (1.5-kg/3½-lb) frozen roasting chicken, defrosted
2 tablespoons corn oil
2 tablespoons lemon juice
½ teaspoon ground turmeric
½ teaspoon ground cardamom
1 teaspoon salt
¼ teaspoon pepper
100 ml/4 fl oz water

Cooking time
1 hour

Skin the chicken. Combine the oil, lemon juice, turmeric, cardamom, salt and pepper in a flameproof casserole. Pour in the water and stir well. Bring to the boil then place the chicken in the casserole, cover tightly and simmer carefully for about 1 hour, until the chicken is tender. Remove the lid to turn the chicken every 15 minutes, adding a little more water if necessary.

Remove the chicken from the pan, spoon over the sauce. Allow to cool. The sauce will set in a golden jelly. Serve with an orange salad.
Serves 4–6

FREEZING HINT

To make a suitable salad to accompany this dish, slice 2 oranges and 1 large radish. Arrange on a bed of lettuce leaves, garnish with mustard and cress and black olives, and spoon over 2 tablespoons of French dressing.

88 Thai festival duck

You will need . . .

1 (2-kg/4½–4¾-lb) frozen duck, defrosted
3 tablespoons clear honey
3 teaspoons soy sauce
1 teaspoon salt
3 tablespoons chicken stock
1 teaspoon ground ginger
1 teaspoon ground coriander
For the side dish:
2 oranges
50 g/2 oz salted cashew nuts
150 ml/5 fl oz natural yogurt
When serving:
fresh orange slices
watercress

Cooking time
2 hours

Oven setting
160°C, 325°F, Gas Mark 3
220°C, 425°F, Gas Mark 7

Place the duck in a large shallow bowl. Mix together the remaining ingredients and pour over the duck. Allow to stand for at least 1 hour, turning the duck occasionally.

Remove the duck from the bowl and place on a grid in a roasting tin. Pour 4 tablespoons of water into the tin. Roast in a moderate oven for about 2 hours, until tender. Spoon out the pan juices and increase the oven heat to hot for the last 20 minutes to crisp the skin.

Meanwhile, prepare the side dish. Slice the oranges thinly and remove the rind with scissors. Arrange the slices on individual side plates. Combine the nuts with the yogurt and spoon over the fruit. Garnish the hot duck with orange slices and watercress and serve accompanied by the side dish.
Serves 4

FREEZING HINT

For parties, a cold boned stuffed chicken or duck looks and tastes good. Make special multi-colour stuffings, using cooked rice, finely diced canned pimento and pistachio nuts. Defrost and slice up while the bird is still chilled for a spectacular result.

Roast duck
89 with grapefruit

Stir-fried
90 turkey with celery

You will need . . .

4 duck portions
salt and pepper
1 large onion, sliced
150 ml/¼ pint grapefruit juice
150 ml/¼ pint strong chicken stock
1 tablespoon cornflour
8 glacé cherries, chopped
When serving:
fresh grapefruit segments
few whole glacé cherries
1 tablespoon chopped parsley
sprigs of watercress

Cooking time
1¼ hours

Oven setting
220°C, 425°F, Gas Mark 7
190°C, 375°F, Gas Mark 5

Storage time
4–6 months

Defrosting time
4 hours at room temperature
and 25 minutes in the oven

Sprinkle the duck portions with seasoning. Arrange close together and skin side down in an ovenproof dish. Place in a hot oven for 15 minutes, turning the portions skin side uppermost after 10 minutes. Pour off any fat. Add the onion slices, pour over the grapefruit juice, cover and bake in a moderately hot oven for 45 minutes, until tender.

Drain the juices into a saucepan, add the stock and bring to the boil. Moisten the cornflour with 1 tablespoon water. Add to the pan and stir until the sauce is smooth and thickened. Season. Stir in the cherries and cool.

To freeze: Pack the portions in a foil container and spoon over the sauce. Seal and label.
To serve: Uncover to defrost. Reheat in a moderately hot oven for 25 minutes. Serve garnished with grapefruit segments, glacé cherries, parsley and watercress, accompanied by a grapefruit salad.
Serves 4

FREEZING HINT

To make a quick grapefruit salad, cut two large ripe grapefruit in half, scoop out the flesh into lettuce cups, mix the juices with an equal quantity of French dressing and pour over the fruit.

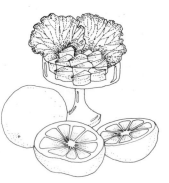

You will need . . .

450 g/1 lb boneless raw turkey
5 sticks celery
2 tablespoons oil
75 g/3 oz mushrooms, sliced
1 tablespoon soy sauce
salt and pepper
1 tablespoon cornflour
4 tablespoons chicken stock
When serving:
chopped parsley

Cooking time
about 15 minutes

Storage time
4–6 months

Defrosting time
25 minutes in boiling water from frozen

Cut the turkey into slices. String the celery and cut into short lengths.

Heat the oil in a large frying pan and use to fry the turkey slices briskly for about 5 minutes, stirring all the time. Add the celery, mushrooms and soy sauce and season with a little salt and pepper. Cook for a further 5 minutes, stirring frequently.

Blend the cornflour with the stock, add to the mixture in the frying pan and bring to the boil, stirring constantly. Simmer for 2 minutes. Cool.

To freeze: Pack in a boiling bag. Seal and label.
To serve: Place the bag, still frozen, in a pan of boiling water, bring back to the boil and simmer for 25 minutes. Serve garnished with parsley.
Serves 4

FREEZING HINT

Using a heat sealer rather than a twist tie produces flat packs which take up the minimum space and are easy to store.

You will need . . .

4 chicken breasts, boned and skinned
salt and pepper
4 thin slices ham
1 (175-g/6-oz) jar cranberry sauce
seasoned flour for coating
40 g/1½ oz butter
150 ml/¼ pint red wine
1 tablespoon cornflour
When serving:
toasted flaked almonds

Cooking time
about 1¼ hours

Oven setting
180°C, 350°F, Gas Mark 4

Storage time
4–6 months

Defrosting time
25 minutes in boiling water
from frozen

Place the chicken breasts between foil and bat out thinly. Sprinkle with seasoning. Top each with a slice of ham and 2 teaspoons of cranberry sauce. Tuck in the ends, roll up tightly and tie with thread. Coat with seasoned flour. Melt the butter and brown on all sides. Remove to a shallow ovenproof casserole. Add the wine and remaining cranberry sauce to the juices in the pan and heat to boiling point, stirring well. Pour over the chicken, cover and cook in a moderate oven for 1 hour.

Place the chicken rolls in 2 foil containers and remove the threads. Pour the juices into a saucepan. Moisten the cornflour with a little cold water, stir into the saucepan and bring to the boil, stirring, until the sauce thickens. Spoon over the chicken and cool.

To freeze: Cover containers with lid or foil. Seal and label.
To serve: Uncover to defrost then reheat in a moderate oven for 25 minutes. Sprinkle with toasted flaked almonds.
Serves 4

FREEZING HINT

Fruits such as elderberries are good to freeze for wine-making later, and the freezing makes them easier to pulp.

You will need . . .

450 g/1 lb boneless raw turkey
150 ml/¼ pint strong chicken stock
1 (225-g/8-oz) can peach slices
1 tablespoon lemon juice
1 tablespoon soy sauce
1 tablespoon tomato ketchup
1 tablespoon peach chutney
½ teaspoon dried basil
salt and pepper
When serving:
watercress

Cooking time
10–15 minutes

Storage time
4–6 months

Defrosting time
25 minutes in boiling
water from frozen

Cut the turkey into large dice and poach in the stock for about 5 minutes, until just tender. Drain and finely chop the peach slices, reserving the syrup.

Place the chopped peaches, peach syrup, lemon juice, soy sauce, tomato ketchup and peach chutney in a pan and stir well. Add the basil and bring slowly to the boil. Stir in the cooked turkey and any remaining stock.

Moisten the cornflour with a little cold water, add to the pan and bring to the boil, stirring constantly. Cook for a further 3 minutes until the sauce is smooth and thickened. Add salt and pepper to taste. Cool.

To freeze: Pack in a boiling bag. Seal and label.
To serve: Place the bag, still frozen, in a pan of boiling water and simmer for 25 minutes. Garnish with watercress and serve with fluffy boiled rice, if liked.
Serves 3–4

FREEZING HINT

When packing fruit for freezing, put some in pickling syrup to serve with cold meats. Peaches and cherries are ideal.

Pastries and puddings

Pastry freezes well in all its many delicious forms. Besides the familiar shortcrust, try your hand at suet, crumble and choux pastries. Quick and easy to make, between them they produce an attractive choice of sweet and savoury tarts, flans, pasties and pies. Puff pastry, more troublesome to make, is readily available in frozen packs, and can be successfully used for recipes such as the old farmhouse favourite, Beehive apples.

As for the puddings, baked or steamed, the results are so delicious you will probably want to double or treble the quantities and freeze away extra supplies.

Garlic and 94 herb crumble pie

93 Crunch-topped coley

(illustrated on frontispiece)

You will need . . .

Cooking time
about 30 minutes

Oven setting
180°C, 350°F, Gas Mark 4
200°C, 400°F, Gas Mark 6

Storage time
4–6 months

Defrosting time
4 hours at room temperature
and 30 minutes in the oven

600 g/1¼ lb coley fillet, skinned
1 medium onion, sliced
salt and pepper
300 ml/½ pint tomato juice
75 g/3 oz butter or margarine
25 g/1 oz flour
1 tablespoon oil
4 large slices white bread, cubed
When serving:
chopped parsley

Layer the fish with the onion in a greased 1-litre/1¾-pint foil pie dish. Season, pour over the tomato juice, cover and cook in a moderate oven for 15 minutes.

Melt 25 g/1 oz butter in a saucepan and stir in the flour. Gradually add the tomato liquid from the fish and bring to the boil, stirring. Season, pour over the fish and onion. Heat the oil and remaining butter and fry the bread cubes until browned. Drain and spoon over the fish mixture.

To freeze: Open freeze until solid then cover with foil or a polythene bag. Seal and label.
To serve: Uncover to defrost, then place in a moderately hot oven for 30 minutes. Garnish with chopped parsley.
Serves 4

You will need . . .

Cooking time
about 20 minutes

Oven setting
200°C, 400°F, Gas Mark 6

Storage time
4–6 months

Defrosting time
4 hours at room temperature
and 30 minutes in the oven

1 tablespoon oil
1 large onion, chopped
1 clove garlic, crushed
350 g/12 oz minced beef
2 teaspoons tomato purée
1 teaspoon sugar
1 beef stock cube
1 tablespoon gravy powder
salt and pepper
6 tablespoons parsley and thyme
    stuffing mix
50 g/2 oz butter or margarine
50 g/2 oz Cheddar cheese, grated

Heat the oil and fry the onion and garlic gently. Add the minced beef and cook until it changes colour, stirring occasionally. Add the tomato purée, sugar and crumbled stock cube and stir well. Cook gently for 10 minutes. Moisten the gravy powder with 2 tablespoons cold water, stir into the meat mixture and bring to the boil, stirring constantly. Season. Turn the mixture into a 1-litre/1¾-pint pie dish or individual ovenproof dishes.

Place the stuffing mix in a bowl, rub in the fat and stir in the cheese. Sprinkle over the meat. Cool.

To freeze: Cover with foil. Seal and label.
To serve: Uncover to defrost, then place in a moderately hot oven for 30 minutes. Garnish with tomato slices and parsley and serve with sweetcorn and baked tomatoes.
Serves 4

FREEZING HINT

Strong freezer bags which seem to have a lingering smell after use may be improved by using a small spoonful of dry mustard dissolved in very hot water to wash them. When turned inside out and dried over a clean milk bottle the smell often vanishes.

FREEZING HINT

Foil covers on pudding basins or pie dishes can become torn or punctured in the freezer, so it is a wise precaution to slip the covered dish into a polythene bag to give extra protection. Remove the bag before reheating.

95 Spiced apple crumble

You will need . . .

Oven setting
200°C, 400°F, Gas Mark 6

Storage time
4–6 months

Defrosting time
50 minutes in the oven
from frozen

450 g/1 lb peeled apple slices
50 g/2 oz sultanas
3 tablespoons water
75 g/3 oz castor sugar
pinch ground cloves
pinch ground cinnamon
225 g/8 oz flour
100 g/4 oz butter or margarine
100 g/4 oz demerara sugar
When serving:
apple slices

Place the apples and sultanas in a greased deep pie dish or foil container and pour over the water. Mix together the castor sugar, cloves and cinnamon and sprinkle over the fruit.

Place the flour in a bowl and rub in the butter until crumbly. Stir in almost all of the demerara sugar.

Spoon the crumble mixture over the prepared fruit to cover it completely. Sprinkle the remaining sugar on top.

To freeze: Cover dish with lid and secure with freezer tape, or cover container with lid or foil. Seal and label
To serve: Uncover and cook from frozen in a moderately hot oven for about 50 minutes, until the crumble is golden brown. Garnish with fresh apple slices.
Serves 4

FREEZING HINT

Crumbles can be baked from frozen with other dishes requiring different oven heats. In a moderate oven allow 1 hour cooking time, in a hot oven about 45 minutes.

96 Prune crumble bars

You will need . . .

Cooking time
about 1 hour

Oven setting
180°C, 350°F, Gas Mark 4

Storage time
4–6 months

Defrosting time
2–3 hours at room
temperature

225 g/8 oz cooked prunes
50 g/2 oz sugar
1 teaspoon grated orange zest
1 tablespoon orange juice
75 g/3 oz plain flour
pinch salt
75 g/3 oz brown sugar
75 g/3 oz rolled oats
150 g/ 5 oz margarine

Stone the prunes and chop the flesh. Mix with the sugar, orange zest and juice in a saucepan and cook over gentle heat, stirring occasionally, until thick. Cool.

Meanwhile, mix together the flour, salt, brown sugar and oats and rub in the fat until the mixture is crumbly.

Press half the crumble mixture into an 18-cm/7-inch square tin and cover with the prune filling. Sprinkle over the remaining crumble mixture and bake in a moderate oven for 45–50 minutes, until golden brown. Cool in the tin and cut into bars when cold.

To freeze: Pack in rigid containers in separated layers. Seal and label.
To serve: Unpack while frozen and spread out on a serving dish to defrost.
Makes about 12

FREEZING HINT

Separate bags of frozen crumble mixture and frozen fruit (such as rhubarb) can be assembled in a greased pie dish and baked immediately without defrosting.

97 Basic choux puffs

You will need . . .

Cooking time
about 30 minutes

Oven setting
190°C, 375°F, Gas Mark 5

Storage time
3–4 months

Defrosting time
5–7 minutes in the oven
from frozen

150 ml/¼ pint water
50 g/2 oz butter
pinch salt
65 g/2½ oz plain flour
2 eggs
When serving:
300 ml/½ pint double cream, whipped
300 ml/½ pint Chocolate marshmallow
  sauce (see recipe 214)

Heat the water, butter and salt in a saucepan until the butter melts. Remove from the heat, stir in all the flour, then beat over a low heat until smooth and the mixture leaves the sides of the pan clean. Cool slightly then beat in the eggs, one at a time. Place small balls of the paste well apart on lightly greased baking trays.

Bake in a moderately hot oven for 20–25 minutes, until well puffed and golden brown. Pierce the puffs with a sharp knife and cool on a wire tray.

To freeze: Pack in a polythene bag. Seal and label.
To serve: Place frozen puffs on baking trays. Reheat and crisp in a moderately hot oven for 5–7 minutes. Cool and fill with the whipped cream, piping if liked. Pile up and pour over the hot chocolate marshmallow sauce.
Makes 15–20
Note: If preferred, substitute your own favourite chocolate sauce recipe.

FREEZING HINT

Pipe out éclair shapes or round puffs of choux paste and open freeze. Pack in layers, and when required arrange on ungreased baking trays and bake from frozen for 5 minutes longer than usual.

98 Orange profiteroles

You will need . . .

Cooking time
20–25 minutes

Oven setting
190°C, 375°F, Gas Mark 5

Storage time
3–4 months

Defrosting time
3 hours at room temperature

1 quantity basic choux paste (see
  recipe 97)
2 tablespoons icing sugar, sifted
1 tablespoon frozen orange concentrate
150 ml/¼ pint double cream, whipped
2 tablespoons Cointreau
When serving:
4 tablespoons water
8 tablespoons sugar

Place teaspoons of the choux paste well apart on lightly greased baking trays and bake in a moderately hot oven for 20–25 minutes. Cool on a wire tray.

Beat together the icing sugar and orange concentrate then gradually fold into the whipped cream with the Cointreau.

Pierce the puffs with a sharp knife and fill with the flavoured cream, piping if wished.

To freeze: Pack carefully in a polythene container. Seal and label.
To serve: Uncover to defrost and pile the puffs in a serving dish. Place the water and sugar in a saucepan and stir until the sugar has dissolved. Bring to the boil without stirring and cook until golden brown. Trickle the caramel over the puffs.
Makes 15–20

FREEZING HINT

Choux puff cases can be filled with savoury as well as sweet mixtures. Thick cheese sauce well-seasoned with mustard is delicious, and you can sprinkle puffs with onion or celery salt before baking for savoury use.

Spotted Dick
99 with apricot sauce

You will need . . .

225 g/8 oz self-raising flour
100 g/ 4 oz shredded suet
50 g/2 oz mixed dried fruit
25 g/1 oz sugar
about 150 ml/¼ pint water
When serving:
4 tablespoons apricot jam
2 tablespoons water

Cooking time
45–50 minutes

Oven setting
190°C, 375°F, Gas Mark 5

Storage time
4–6 months

Defrosting time
40 minutes in the oven from frozen

Mix the dry ingredients together and stir in the water to form a dough. Shape into a roll and wrap loosely in greased foil. Bake in a moderately hot oven for 45–50 minutes. Cool.

To freeze: Wrap in foil. Seal and label.
To serve: Place still frozen and wrapped in a moderately hot oven for 30 minutes. Uncover the top and return to the oven for a further 10 minutes. Heat the jam and water together and sieve. Serve hot poured over the spotted dick.
Serves 4–6

100 Light fruit pudding

You will need . . .

100 g/4 oz self-raising flour
½ teaspoon ground mixed spice
100 g/4 oz soft brown breadcrumbs
75 g/3 oz shredded suet
100 g/4 oz soft brown sugar
100 g/4 oz mixed dried fruit
2 eggs, beaten
2 tablespoons orange marmalade
1 tablespoon milk
When serving:
golden syrup

Cooking time
2½–3 hours

Storage time
4–6 months

Defrosting time
1¼ hours in boiling water from frozen

Sift the flour with the mixed spice into a bowl and stir in the breadcrumbs, suet and sugar.

Sprinkle in the dried fruit and add the beaten eggs combined with the marmalade. Stir in sufficient milk to give a soft dropping consistency.

Turn the mixture into a greased 1-litre/1¾-pint foil pudding basin. Cover and steam for 2½–3 hours. Cool.

To freeze: Cover with fresh foil and pack in a polythene bag. Seal and label.
To serve: Remove the polythene bag and place the pudding, still frozen and covered, in a saucepan. Pour in boiling water to come one third up the sides of the basin and steam for 1¼ hours. Serve with warmed golden syrup.
Serves 4–6

FREEZING HINT

Leftover Christmas pudding can be frozen. Cut into thick slices and pack in foil. Reheat in the oven. Slices frozen with dividers can be fried from frozen in hot butter.

FREEZING HINT

In these diet-conscious days, not every member of the family can enjoy steamed sponge or suet puddings. Make a large plain pudding and cut it into wedges. When cold, wrap the wedges individually in foil. The parcels can be reheated in the oven to serve with a variety of toppings.

101 Raisin and cheese pie

You will need . . .

Cooking time
1 hour

Oven setting
200°C, 400°F, Gas Mark 6
180°C, 350°F, Gas Mark 4

Storage time
4–6 months

Defrosting time
4 hours at room temperature
and 25 minutes in the oven

275 g/10 oz flour
pinch salt
65 g/2½ oz margarine
65 g/2½ oz lard
2 tablespoons cold water
For the filling:
50 g/2 oz seedless raisins
2 eggs
1 tablespoon milk
salt and pepper
pinch cayenne pepper
175 g/6 oz Cheddar cheese, grated
pinch dried mixed herbs
beaten egg to brush

Sift the flour and salt into a bowl and rub in the fats. Add the water and mix to a firm dough. Knead lightly. This makes a 275 g/10 oz quantity of shortcrust pastry.

Roll out half the pastry to line a 20-cm/8-inch foil pie plate. Sprinkle the raisins over the base. Beat the eggs with the milk, seasoning and cayenne. Stir in the cheese and herbs and pour into the lined pie plate. Roll out the remaining pastry to cover. Dampen the edges and seal. Decorate with pastry trimmings and brush with the beaten egg. Bake in a moderately hot oven for 30 minutes, then reduce to moderate for a further 30 minutes. Cool.

To freeze: Cover with foil. Seal and label.
To serve: Uncover to defrost, then reheat in a moderately hot oven. Serve hot, garnished with parsley.
Serves 4–6

FREEZING HINT

Prepare shortcrust pastry in bulk using 1 kg/2¼ lb flour, 275 g/10 oz lard, 225 g/8 oz margarine, and cold water to mix. You should get 2 flans, 2 double-crust pies and 12 small tarts from this amount.

Apple 102 and bacon churdles

You will need . . .

Cooking time
about 1 hour

Oven setting
190°C, 375°F, Gas Mark 5
180°C, 350°F, Gas Mark 4

Storage time
3–4 months

Defrosting time
35 minutes in the oven from frozen

350 g/12 oz bacon pieces, derinded
1 large onion, chopped
175 g/6 oz pig's liver, sliced
2 large cooking apples
¼ teaspoon dried sage
salt and freshly ground black pepper
450 g/1 lb shortcrust pastry
3 tablespoons dry white breadcrumbs
25 g/1 oz Cheddar cheese, grated
1 tablespoon milk

Fry the bacon gently with the onion until the fat runs. Add the liver and fry until firm. Mince this mixture. Peel, core and chop the apples and stir in with the sage and seasoning.

Roll out the pastry and cut into eight 15-cm/6-inch circles. Spoon on the filling, dampen the edges of the pastry and bring up around the filling. Join together over the top, leaving the centre open. Place on a baking tray. Mix the breadcrumbs and cheese, sprinkle over the exposed fillings, then brush the pastry with milk. Bake in a moderately hot oven for 45–55 minutes. Cool.

To freeze: Pack individually in foil, then together in a rigid container. Seal and label.
To serve: Reheat from frozen, wrapped in foil, in a moderately hot oven for 20 minutes. Uncover and heat for a further 15 minutes. Serve with a salad.
Makes 8

FREEZING HINT

Unblanched apple slices packed dry in sugar do discolour but go a lovely golden brown and are good for dishes such as Apple Amber.

103 Iced Camembert tart

Deep dish
104 strawberry pie

You will need . . .

Cooking time
40 minutes

Oven setting
190°C, 375°F, Gas Mark 5

Storage time
6 months

Defrosting time
4 hours at room temperature

225 g/8 oz shortcrust pastry
15 g/½ oz gelatine
2 tablespoons hot water
3 eggs, separated
150 ml/¼ pint single cream
1 ripe Camembert cheese
When serving:
parsley
sliced tomatoes

You will need . . .

Oven setting
200°C, 400°F, Gas Mark 6
180°C, 350°F, Gas Mark 4

Storage time
4–6 months

Defrosting time
35–40 minutes in the oven
from frozen

175 g/6 oz sugar
25 g/1 oz flour
pinch salt
1 kg/2¼ lb strawberries
25 g/1 oz butter
225 g/8 oz shortcrust pastry
When serving:
1 tablespoon milk
little castor sugar

Roll out the pastry to line a 20-cm/8-inch flan dish, and bake blind for 30 minutes in a moderately hot oven. Cool. Meanwhile, dissolve the gelatine in the water and cool.

Beat together the egg yolks and cream in a small bowl, then stand over a pan of hot water and cook, stirring constantly, until thick. Trim away the outer crust from the cheese. Cut the cheese into small dice, add to the egg mixture and stir until dissolved. Remove from the heat and stir in the gelatine. Whisk the egg whites until stiff, fold into the cheese mixture, and pour into the cooled flan case.

To freeze: Open freeze the flan, then wrap in foil to make a parcel. Seal and label.
To serve: Open the parcel to defrost. Serve cut in wedges, garnished with parsley and tomatoes.
Serves 4–6

Mix together the sugar, flour and salt. Arrange the strawberries in a 1-litre/1¾-pint ovenproof or foil pie dish, sprinkling over the sugar mixture. Dot with pieces of butter.

Roll out the pastry and cut a lid for the pie.

Roll out the pastry trimmings and cut a strip to fit the rim of the dish, dampen it and press into place. Brush this strip with water. Lift the pastry lid over the fruit, seal the edges well together and flute.

To freeze: Open freeze until solid then cover with foil or a polythene bag. Seal and label.
To serve: Uncover and brush pastry with milk. Bake from frozen in a moderately hot oven for 25 minutes. Lower oven temperature to moderate and continue cooking for a further 10–15 minutes, until golden brown. Sprinkle with castor sugar before serving.
Serves 4–6

FREEZING HINT

Pastry trimmings need not be thrown away. Stamp out small shapes with a fancy cutter, sprinkle with coloured coffee sugar, or with grated cheese, salt and pepper, and bake in a hot oven for 8–10 minutes. Cool, and store in small bags to use as decorations or garnishes.

FREEZING HINT

Double crust pastry pies, containing a cooked meat or raw fruit filling, can be frozen with raw pastry. By the time the pastry is cooked, the meat filling will be reheated or the fruit filling cooked.

105 Beehive apples

You will need . . .

Cooking time
20–25 minutes

Oven setting
200°C, 400°F, Gas Mark 6

Storage time
4–6 months

Defrosting time
2 hours at room temperature
and 15 minutes in the oven

4 small cooking apples
50 g/2 oz sultanas
25 g/1 oz ground almonds
4 tablespoons orange jelly marmalade
450 g/1 lb frozen puff pastry,
    defrosted
1 egg, beaten
When serving:
25 g/1 oz butter
4 tablespoons orange jelly marmalade

Peel and core the apples. Mix together the sultanas, ground almonds and marmalade and use to fill the centres of the apples.

Roll out the pastry thinly to a rectangle and cut into strips 1 cm/½ inch wide. Wrap round each apple, until the whole apple is covered and it looks like a beehive. Place on a baking tray.

Brush the apple beehives all over with beaten egg and bake in a moderately hot oven for 20–25 minutes, until golden brown. Cool.

To freeze: Pack in a rigid container. Seal and label.
To serve: Unpack and arrange on a baking tray to defrost, then reheat in a moderately hot oven for 15 minutes. Meanwhile, place the butter and marmalade in a saucepan and heat gently, stirring frequently, until both are melted. Serve the hot beehive apples with the marmalade sauce.
Serves 4

FREEZING HINT

When preparing apples for freezing, save the skins and cores and freeze these in polythene bags. They can be used for making apple jelly or to add to other fruits for jelly-making which have a lower pectin content.

Chicken liver
106 and bacon triangles

You will need . . .

Cooking time
about 35 minutes

Oven setting
220°C, 425°F, Gas Mark 7

Storage time
3–4 months

Defrosting time
12–15 minutes in the oven
from frozen

4 rashers streaky bacon
175 g/6 oz chicken livers
salt and pepper
2 tablespoons brown gravy
1 tablespoon apricot or peach chutney
450 g/1 lb frozen puff pastry, defrosted
1 egg, beaten

Derind and finely chop the bacon. Roughly chop the chicken livers. Fry the bacon until the fat runs. Add the chicken livers, season and stir over moderate heat until just firm. Add the gravy and chutney and cool.

Roll out the pastry thinly and cut into 12 (10-cm/ 4-inch) squares. Spoon the filling into the centres. Brush the edges with beaten egg, fold over diagonally to make triangular puffs and press the edges well together. Brush the tops with the remaining beaten egg, place on a dampened baking tray and bake in a hot oven for 20–25 minutes, until well risen and golden brown. Cool.

To freeze: Pack in a polythene container in layers with dividers. Seal and label.
To serve: Unpack, place still frozen on a baking tray then heat in a hot oven for 12–15 minutes.
Makes 12

FREEZING HINT

To make a quick party special, roll out puff pastry thinly, to a 30-cm/ 12-inch square. Spread with savoury white sauce, scatter with chopped anchovies, open freeze and pack. When required, bake from frozen in a hot oven for 15 minutes.

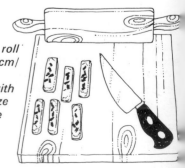

107 Puff cheese whirls

You will need . . .

225 g/8 oz frozen puff pastry, defrosted
50 g/2 oz blue cheese
40 g/1½ oz cream cheese
1 teaspoon Worcestershire sauce
good pinch cayenne pepper

Cooking time
10–12 minutes

Oven setting
220°C, 425°F, Gas Mark 7

Storage time
4–6 months

Defrosting time
1 hour at room temperature

Roll out the pastry thinly to an oblong about 30 × 20 cm/
12 × 8 inches. Crumble the blue cheese into a basin and
beat in the cream cheese, Worcestershire sauce and
cayenne. Spread this mixture evenly over the pastry and
roll up tightly starting from one long edge, like a Swiss
roll. Chill until firm.

Cut the roll into 5-mm/¼-inch slices and lay these flat
and well apart on non-stick baking trays, or baking trays
lined with non-stick paper.

Bake in a hot oven for 10–12 minutes, or until golden
brown. Cool and remove to a wire tray before completely
cold.

To freeze: Pack in a polythene container in layers with
dividers. Seal and label.
To serve: Unpack while still frozen and arrange on a
serving dish to defrost.
Makes 20–24

FREEZING HINT

*It saves time and trouble to heat-
seal boiling bags containing lightly
cooked steaks or fillets of white
fish in a simple sauce, so that the
bag can be snipped after heating
in boiling water, and the serving
pressed out on a plate.*

108 Turkey ladder puff

You will need . . .

25 g/1 oz butter
1 medium onion, chopped
300 ml/½ pint whisked savoury sauce
  (see recipe 210: made to a binding
  consistency with 50 g/2 oz butter,
50 g/2 oz flour and 300 ml/½ pint milk)
275 g/10 oz cooked turkey, diced
2 small gherkins, sliced
salt and pepper
225 g/8 oz frozen puff pastry, defrosted
When serving:
1 egg, beaten

Cooking time
about 10 minutes

Oven setting
220°C, 425°F, Gas Mark 7
190°C, 375°F, Gas Mark 5

Storage time
4–6 months

Defrosting time
45–50 minutes in the oven
from frozen

Melt the butter and fry the onion. Stir in the white sauce
then the turkey, gherkins and seasoning to taste. Cool.

Roll out the pastry to a 30-cm/12-inch square and cut
in half. Place one half on a baking tray and spread the
turkey filling down the centre. Fold the remaining piece
of pastry in half lengthways. Leaving a 5-cm/2-inch margin
at each end, cut the folded edge at 2.5-cm/1-inch intervals
to within 2.5 cm/1 inch of the opposite edges. Place over
the turkey base, dampen the edges and press well together
to seal.

To freeze: Open freeze until solid, then pack in foil or a
polythene bag. Seal and label.
To serve: Uncover, place on a dampened baking tray,
brush with egg and bake in a hot oven for 30 minutes.
Reduce to moderately hot and bake for a further 15–20
minutes. Serve with salad.
Serves 4

FREEZING HINT

*Frozen puff pastry will rise more
evenly if pricked with a thin
skewer at equal intervals round the
top edge before baking.*

109 Apple brûlée

You will need . . .

Cooking time
about 10 minutes

Storage time
4–6 months

Defrosting time
4–6 hours in the refrigerator
and 5 minutes under the
grill

1 kg/2¼ lb cooking apples
sugar to taste
150 ml/¼ pint double cream
150 ml/¼ pint single cream
grated zest of 1 orange
When serving:
soft brown sugar

Cut up the apples and cook with sugar to taste and a little
water. When quite soft press through a sieve. There
should be about 600 ml/1 pint apple purée.

Pour the purée into an ovenproof serving dish. Cool.

Place the creams together in a basin and whip until
thick. Stir in the orange zest and spread the cream over the
apple purée.

To freeze: Cover with lid or foil. Seal and label.
To serve: Uncover to defrost. Cover surface of cream
with a thick layer of sugar and place under a hot grill until
the sugar melts and caramelises.
Serves 4

FREEZING HINT

*To make a smooth velvety purée
for freezing, choose Bramley
apples which 'fall' when cooked.
Other varieties of cooking apple
will retain their shape in slices.*

110 Lemon curd pudding

You will need . . .

Cooking time
1½ hours

Storage time
4–6 months

Defrosting time
1 hour in boiling water
from frozen

2 lemons
175 g/6 oz butter
175 g/6 oz castor sugar
2 eggs
100 g/4 oz self-raising flour
2 tablespoons milk

Finely grate the lemon zest and squeeze the juice.

Cream together 100 g/4 oz each of the butter and
sugar until light and fluffy. Beat in 1 egg and the lemon
zest. Add the remaining egg and a little flour and beat well.
Fold in the rest of the flour and the milk with a metal spoon.

Strain the lemon juice and heat in a saucepan with the
remaining butter and sugar until the butter has melted.
Pour into the bottom of a buttered 1-litre/1¾-pint foil
pudding basin, and spoon the pudding mixture over the
top. Cover and steam for 1½ hours. Cool.

To freeze: Cover with fresh foil and pack in a polythene
bag. Seal and label.
To serve: Remove the polythene bag and place the pudding, still frozen and covered, in a saucepan. Pour in
boiling water to come one third up the sides of the basin
and steam for 1 hour. Turn out to serve with the lemon
curd sauce on top.
Serves 4

FREEZING HINT

*Although a foil cover can be used
instead of a pudding cloth or
greaseproof paper, the cover must
be pleated to allow for expansion
of the pudding above the rim of
the basin as it cooks.*

Rich chocolate
111 sponge pudding

You will need . . .

50 g/2 oz plain chocolate
1 tablespoon milk
1 teaspoon instant coffee powder
100 g/4 oz self-raising flour
pinch salt
1 tablespoon cocoa powder
100 g/4 oz butter
100 g/4 oz castor sugar
2 eggs, beaten
2 teaspoons grated orange zest

Cooking time
1½ hours

Storage time
4–6 months

Defrosting time
1 hour in boiling water from frozen

Put the chocolate, milk and coffee powder in a small basin and place this in a pan of hot water until the chocolate has melted. Stir well. Sift together the flour, salt and cocoa.

Cream the butter and sugar until light and fluffy. Gradually add the eggs, beating well after each addition. Stir in the orange zest. Fold in the flour mixture and the chocolate mixture and blend well.

Spoon into a greased 1-litre/1¾-pint foil pudding basin. Cover and steam for 1½ hours. Cool.

To freeze: Cover with fresh foil and pack in a polythene bag. Seal and label.
To serve: Remove the polythene bag and place the pudding, still frozen and covered, in a saucepan. Pour in boiling water to come one third up the sides of the basin and steam for 1 hour. Serve with Chocolate marshmallow sauce (see recipe 214), or with your own favourite chocolate sauce.
Serves 4

FREEZING HINT

Sponge puddings can be frozen uncooked. When required to serve, place frozen in a saucepan and pour in boiling water as above. Steam for 2–3 hours depending on size. Rich chocolate pudding above would take 2¼ hours.

Eve's apple
112 and peach pudding

You will need . . .

450 g/1 lb peeled apple slices
150 g/5 oz castor sugar
1 (425-g/15-oz) can peach slices, drained
75 g/3 oz butter
1 egg, beaten
few drops vanilla essence
100 g/4 oz self-raising flour
When serving:
castor sugar

Oven setting
190°C, 375°F, Gas Mark 5

Storage time
4–6 months

Defrosting time
1–1¼ hours in the oven from frozen

Place the apple slices in the base of a greased baking dish or foil container and sprinkle with 50 g/2 oz of the sugar. Cover with the drained peach slices.

Cream the butter with the remaining sugar until light and fluffy. Gradually beat in the egg and vanilla essence. Fold in the flour.

Spoon this mixture over the apples and peach slices and smooth the top.

To freeze: Open freeze until firm. Cover dish with lid and secure with freezer tape or cover container with lid or foil. Seal and label.
To serve: Uncover and place still frozen in a moderately hot oven for about 1–1¼ hours, until golden brown. Cover with foil if the pudding is becoming too brown. Sprinkle with castor sugar and serve hot with custard or cream.
Serves 4

FREEZING HINT

To make exquisite apple sauce – cook sliced apple in sweet cider, adding a few drops of lemon juice to keep the colour bright. Sweeten to taste and beat in a little melted butter before serving.

113 Pumpkin pie

You will need . . .

Cooking time
40—45 minutes

Oven setting
230°C, 450°F, Gas Mark 8
180°C, 350°F, Gas Mark 4

Storage time
4–6 months

Defrosting time
4 hours at room temperature
and 20 minutes in the oven
if required warm

225 g/8 oz shortcrust pastry
100 g/4 oz light soft brown sugar
good pinch salt
½ teaspoon ground cinnamon
¼ teaspoon ground mace
1 egg, beaten
400 g/14 oz canned or cooked pumpkin
  purée
150 ml/¼ pint whipping cream or
  evaporated milk

Roll out the pastry and use to line a 20-cm/8-inch fluted flan ring or foil flan case. Roll out the trimmings and cut strips to make a lattice topping.

Mix together the sugar, salt, cinnamon, mace and egg and beat well. Add the pumpkin purée and the cream or evaporated milk. Stir well and pour into the prepared pastry case. Decorate the pie with the lattice strips.

Bake in a hot oven for 15 minutes, then reduce heat and continue cooking in a moderate oven for a further 25—30 minutes, until the filling is firm and the pastry golden brown. Cool.

To freeze: Cover with foil. Seal and label.
To serve: Uncover and defrost. If required warm, reheat after defrosting in a moderate oven for 20 minutes.
Serves 4–6

FREEZING HINT

Cover the bottom of an uncooked pastry flan case with a thin layer of jam, if this will go well with the intended filling. It prevents the pastry from becoming soggy.

114 California prune pie

You will need . . .

Cooking time
about 40 minutes

Oven setting
200°C, 400°F, Gas Mark 6

Storage time
4–6 months

Defrosting time
4 hours at room temperature

350 g/12 oz prunes
225 g/8 oz shortcrust pastry
2 eggs
100 g/4 oz soft brown sugar
150 ml/¼ pint soured cream
When serving:
little whipped cream or few miniature
  meringues

Place the prunes in a saucepan, cover with cold water and leave overnight. Lift out the prunes, stone and chop. Boil the soaking water to reduce to 50 ml/2 fl oz.

Meanwhile, roll out the pastry to line a 20-cm/8-inch fluted flan ring or foil flan case. Prick well, line with grease-proof paper or foil and fill with baking beans. Bake 'blind' in a moderately hot oven for 15 minutes. Remove the paper and beans and bake for a further 10 minutes. Cool.

Return the prune pulp to the saucepan with the reduced liquid. Add the eggs, sugar and soured cream and cook over moderate heat for about 10 minutes, stirring all the time, until the mixture thickens. Cool and spoon into the pastry case.

To freeze: Open freeze until firm, then cover with foil or a polythene bag. Seal and label.
To serve: Uncover to defrost then decorate with rosettes of whipped cream or miniature meringues.
Serves 4–6

FREEZING HINT

Blocks of almond paste are easy to buy around Christmas but not always to be found at other times. A block of almond paste straight from the freezer can be grated, and mixed with fruit for a tart or pie.

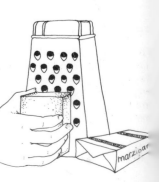

Orange
115 and treacle tart

116 Coconut apple wedge

You will need . . .

225 g/8 oz shortcrust pastry
For the filling:
3 tablespoons black treacle
75 g/3 oz butter
75 g/3 oz castor sugar
1 egg
grated zest and juice of ½ orange
25 g/1 oz ground almonds
100 g/4 oz flour
25 g/1 oz flaked almonds

Cooking time
35–40 minutes

Oven setting
200°C, 400°F, Gas Mark 6
180°C, 350°F, Gas Mark 4

Storage time
4–6 months

Defrosting time
4 hours at room temperature
and 20 minutes in the oven

Roll out the pastry and use to line a 20-cm/8-inch fluted flan ring or foil flan case. Spread with the treacle. Cream the butter and sugar together until light and fluffy. Beat in the egg, grated orange zest and ground almonds. Fold in the flour, alternately with the orange juice, then spread the mixture over the treacle.

Bake in a moderately hot oven for 15 minutes. Reduce the oven heat to moderate. Scatter the flaked almonds over the tart and return it to the moderate oven for a further 20–25 minutes. Cool.

To freeze: Cover with foil or a polythene bag. Seal and label.
To serve: Uncover to defrost, then reheat in a moderately hot oven for 20 minutes.
Serves 4–6

You will need . . .

100 g/4 oz plain flour
50 g/2 oz soft brown sugar
75 g/3 oz butter
2 eggs
100 g/4 oz castor sugar
25 g/1 oz plain flour
½ teaspoon baking powder
½ teaspoon salt
¼–½ teaspoon ground cinnamon
450 g/1 lb dessert apples
50 g/2 oz desiccated coconut
25 g/1 oz nuts, chopped
1 teaspoon vanilla essence

Cooking time
about 1 hour

Oven setting
180°C, 350°F, Gas Mark 4

Storage time
4–6 months

Defrosting time
4 hours at room temperature
and 20 minutes in the oven

Mix 100 g/4 oz flour with the brown sugar and rub in the butter. Press into the base of a 20-cm/8-inch loose-bottomed cake tin. Bake in a moderate oven for 20 minutes.

Whisk the eggs until thick then gradually whisk in the castor sugar. Sift the flour, baking powder, salt and cinnamon and fold in lightly. Peel, core and slice the apples and stir in with the coconut, nuts and vanilla essence. Spread evenly over the prepared crust and bake for 50–60 minutes, covering with foil for the last 15 minutes.

To freeze: Open freeze until solid then remove from the tin and pack in foil. Seal and label.
To serve: Unwrap and defrost. Reheat in a moderate oven for 20 minutes. Sprinkle with castor sugar and serve with hot Lemon butterscotch sauce (see recipe 213).
Serves 4–6

FREEZING HINT

To enable you to serve just the number of wedges required, cut up flans before freezing, and pack each wedge separately. Or divide the flan in half and pack in two parcels, to serve fewer portions.

FREEZING HINT

When making double crust fruit pies, sprinkle a dusting of cornflour mixed with castor sugar over the fruit before putting the lid in place. The cornflour absorbs the juice as the fruit cooks and prevents it from bubbling out through the crust.

Desserts and ice creams

Ice cream remains a firm favourite for dessert, so take your choice from sorbets, fruit ices, sherbets and rich cream ices. All these homemade ice creams are reasonably costed, and some include ingredients which would put them in the luxury class if bought ready-made — crushed ratafia biscuits, liqueurs and nuts. Do try my hot ice cream sweets; including two versions of the famous baked Alaska, and a star performer, Hot 'n' cold cream puffs, where ice cream filled choux puffs are served crisply fried with a delicious sauce.

New recipes for cheesecake are always in demand. There are four to choose from here, two baked and two unbaked, guaranteed to be winners.

117 Apricot bombe

(illustrated on back of jacket)

You will need . . .	2 (44-g/1½-oz) sachets dessert topping mix
	300 ml/½ pint cold milk
Storage time	2 tablespoons castor sugar
4–6 months	25 g/1 oz plain chocolate, melted
Defrosting time	1 (425-g/15-oz) can apricots, drained
30 minutes in the	2 teaspoons brandy
refrigerator	½ teaspoon finely grated orange zest
	2 tablespoons orange juice

Make up 1 sachet of topping mix using half the milk. Whisk in 1 tablespoon sugar and the melted chocolate. Use to line the base and sides of a 1-litre/1¾-pint foil pudding basin and freeze until solid.

Meanwhile, blend the apricots in a liquidiser or sieve. Stir in the brandy, orange zest and juice. Make up the second topping mix using the rest of the milk and whisk in the remaining sugar. Fold the apricot mixture into the topping and spoon into the centre of the frozen chocolate shell.

To freeze: Cover with foil. Seal and label.
To serve: Dip basin in warm water and turn out on to serving plate. Decorate with piped whipped cream and sprinkle toasted flaked almonds on top before softening in the refrigerator.
Serves 6

Chocolate 118 whisky pudding

You will need . . .	2 eggs
	1 tablespoon castor sugar
Storage time	225 g/8 oz unsalted butter, melted
4–6 months	225 g/8 oz plain chocolate, melted
Defrosting time	2 tablespoons whisky
3 hours at room temperature	225 g/8 oz digestive biscuits, crushed
	50 g/2 oz walnuts, chopped
	50 g/2 oz glacé cherries, chopped
	When serving:
	150 ml/¼ pint double cream, whipped
	chocolate drops

Whisk the eggs with the sugar until thick and creamy. Gradually whisk in the melted butter and then the melted chocolate, a little at a time.

Fold in the whisky, biscuit crumbs, nuts and cherries.

Spoon the mixture into a well-oiled, loose-bottomed 18-cm/7-inch cake tin and smooth the top.

To freeze: Open freeze until solid them remove from the tin. Place on a plate or firm base and freeze again until firm. Cover with foil. Seal and label.
To serve: Uncover while still frozen. Defrost and serve at room temperature, decorated with piped whipped cream and chocolate drops.
Serves 4–6

FREEZING HINT

Leftover syrup from canned fruit can be frozen in small polythene containers for future use with fresh fruit salads.

FREEZING HINT

To freeze egg whites, simply pack them leaving a headspace. No beating or addition of a stabiliser is required. Allow the whites to return to room temperature before using, especially for meringues.

119 Strawberry mousse

You will need . . .

Storage time
12 months

Defrosting time
4 hours in the refrigerator
or serve from frozen

600 ml/1 pint strawberry purée
50 g/2 oz cottage cheese, sieved
2 tablespoons castor sugar
15 g/½ oz gelatine
4 tablespoons cold water
150 ml/¼ pint whipping cream
2 egg whites
When serving:
150 ml/¼ pint double cream, whipped
few whole strawberries

Mix together the strawberry purée, cottage cheese and castor sugar. Beat vigorously for 1 minute to combine the ingredients thoroughly. Dissolve the gelatine and water in a bowl over a pan of hot water. Remove from the heat and allow to cool.

Gradually whisk the dissolved gelatine into the strawberry mixture. Allow to stand until it is beginning to set. Whip the cream lightly, and stiffly beat the egg whites.

Fold in the cream, then the egg whites.

To freeze: Divide between 2 large or 8 individual polythene containers. Seal and label.
To serve: Transfer to the refrigerator 4 hours before serving time, or serve like an ice cream in the frozen state. Decorate with swirls of whipped cream and strawberries.
Serves 8
Note: Other fruit purées can be used for this recipe. Raspberry, loganberry and blackcurrant are particularly suitable.

120 Pineapple cream log

You will need . . .

Storage time
4–6 months

Defrosting time
6 hours in the refrigerator

1 (312-g/11-oz) can pineapple cubes
16 ginger biscuits
300 ml/½ pint whipping cream
50 g/2 oz plain chocolate, grated
When serving:
chocolate curls

Drain the pineapple cubes, reserving the syrup. Roughly chop the cubes. Lay the biscuits flat on a plate and sprinkle them with all the pineapple syrup. Whip the cream until thick, reserve two-thirds to coat the roll, and fold the grated chocolate and chopped pineapple into the remainder.

Sandwich the biscuits together, four at a time, with the pineapple cream. Arrange the stacks, on edge, side by side on a sheet of foil. Bring the long sides of the foil together and fold down to make a Swiss roll shape. Fold in the ends tightly. Freeze the parcel for 1 hour.

Remove the foil, place the log on a firm base and spread over the remaining whipped cream to enclose the log completely. Mark with the back of a round-bladed knife and pipe any leftover cream in rosettes along the edges.

To freeze: Open freeze until firm then cover with a polythene container. Seal and label.
To serve: Uncover to defrost. Decorate with large curls of chocolate, made by scraping a potato peeler along the flat side of a block of chocolate. Serve cut in slices.
Serves 6

FREEZING HINT

To make refreshing apple juice — cut up and boil 1 kg/generous 2 lb eating apples in 300 ml/½ pint water until pulped. Leftovers from preparing apple slices for freezing can also be used. Strain the pulp through a bag and freeze as cubes, without sweetening.

FREEZING HINT

When making a cake or dessert using canned fruit, freeze a few well-shaped pieces of fruit in a small container to decorate the cake after defrosting.

121 Simple baked Alaska

You will need . . .

Oven setting
220°C, 425°F, Gas Mark 7

Storage time
3 months

Defrosting time
5–6 minutes in the oven
from frozen

100 g/4 oz stale cake or trifle sponges
2 tablespoons Marsala or sweet sherry
2 tablespoons apricot jam
3 egg whites
175 g/6 oz castor sugar
500 ml/17·5 fl oz vanilla ice cream

Cut the cake into slices and use to cover the base of a
shallow ovenproof dish or foil plate. Fit the pieces closely
together. Sprinkle the cake with the Marsala or sherry and
spread with the jam.

Place the egg whites in a basin and whisk until stiff.
Gradually whisk in half the sugar and continue whisking
until the mixture is glossy and standing in peaks. Fold in
the remaining sugar.

Mound up the ice cream on the prepared base, leaving
a margin of uncovered cake round the edge. Swirl the
meringue over the whole cake, to completely cover it.

To freeze: Open freeze until firm then cover lightly with
cling film and label. The meringue always remains quite
soft so protect with an inverted polythene container or
basin if possible.
To serve: Uncover and place immediately in a hot oven
for 5–6 minutes, until the meringue is golden brown.
Serves 6

FREEZING HINT

*For a special occasion, soak the
sponge with cherry brandy and use
drained and stoned canned black
cherries under the ice cream.*

122 Orange Alaska cups

You will need . . .

Oven setting
230°C, 450°F, Gas Mark 8

Storage time
3 months

Defrosting time
4 minutes in the oven from
frozen

4 large oranges
4 tablespoons sherry
500 ml/17·5 fl oz vanilla ice cream
3 egg whites
50 g/2 oz castor sugar
2 tablespoons icing sugar, sifted

Make sure you have space in the freezer for a baking tray.
Grate a little zest from both ends of the oranges. Trim
a thin slice of peel away with the grated parts, so that the
oranges will stand firmly when halved. Cut carefully in
half. Scoop out the flesh and mix with the sherry. Leave to
stand for a few minutes. Remove pith from the orange
halves. Soften the ice cream slightly and combine with
the orange mixture. Fill the orange halves, pressing down
well and mounding up in the centres. Space out evenly
on the baking tray. Beat the egg whites stiffly, add the
castor sugar and orange zest and beat again. Fold in the
sifted icing sugar. Pipe or spoon the meringue over the
ice cream, completely covering it.

To freeze: Open freeze on the tray until firm, which will
take about 2 hours. Then transfer to a large polythene
container just deep enough to clear the meringue tops
when sealed. Seal and label.
To serve: Place the number of cups required on a baking
tray, put into a hot oven for 4 minutes and serve at once.
Serves 8

FREEZING HINT

*Freezer owners who buy ice cream
in 4-litre containers can put the
empty containers to all sorts of
uses. They make especially pretty
wastepaper baskets, given two
coats of emulsion paint or
covered with vinyl wallpaper.*

123 Iced mocha meringue

Hot 'n' cold
124 cream puffs

You will need . . .

	100 g/4 oz leftover chocolate cake
	3 tablespoons coffee liqueur
Oven setting	3 egg whites
220°C, 425°F, Gas Mark 7	175 g/6 oz castor sugar
	500 ml/17.5 fl oz chocolate ice cream
Storage time	25 g/1 oz chocolate drops
3 months	

Defrosting time
4–5 minutes in the oven from frozen

Slice the cake and use to line a shallow ovenproof dish or foil plate. Sprinkle with the coffee liqueur.

Whisk the egg whites until stiff then add half the sugar and continue whisking for about 1 minute, until the mixture is glossy. Fold in the remaining sugar with a metal spoon.

Mound up the ice cream on the cake base, keeping it away from the edges. Cover the ice cream with chocolate drops, then completely cover the cake with the meringue mixture.

To freeze: Open freeze until firm then cover lightly with cling film and label. The outside remains soft even when frozen, so protect as for Simple baked Alaska.
To serve: Unwrap and place still frozen in a hot oven for 4–5 minutes, until the meringue is golden brown.
Serves 6

You will need . . .

	16 choux puffs (see recipe 97)
	500 ml/17.5 fl oz vanilla ice cream
Cooking time	*When serving:*
15–20 minutes	100 g/4 oz plain flour
	1 teaspoon sugar
Oven setting	$\frac{1}{4}$ teaspoon salt
190°C, 375°F, Gas Mark 5	1 egg, beaten
	250 ml/ 8 fl oz pineapple juice
Storage time	oil for frying
3–4 months	castor sugar for sprinkling
	For the sauce:
Defrosting	1 (376-g/13$\frac{1}{4}$-oz) can crushed pineapple
Fry the puffs from frozen in	1 tablespoon golden syrup
hot oil while the sauce	2 teaspoons arrowroot
cooks	

Bake the choux puffs in a moderately hot oven, pierce and allow to cool. Chill and fill with the ice cream.

To freeze: Open freeze until hard then pack in a rigid container. Seal and label.
To serve: Sift the flour, sugar and salt into a bowl and beat in the egg and fruit juice. Unpack the frozen puffs, a few at a time, quickly dip in the batter and fry in deep hot oil for 1–2 minutes, until crisp and golden. Sprinkle with castor sugar. Meanwhile, turn the crushed pineapple and its juice into a saucepan, stir in the golden syrup and heat. Stir in the arrowroot, moistened with a little cold water, bring to the boil, stirring, and cook gently until the sauce is clear and slightly thickened. Serve with the ice cream puffs.
Serves 4

FREEZING HINT

When you have only chocolate ice cream in the freezer, you may be glad to try this quick sauce to serve with it. Put 12 marshmallows with 2 tablespoons lemon juice in a basin over hot water, allow to melt and serve as a topping on scoops of the ice cream.

FREEZING HINT

When labelling packs for storage, remember to put labels on the side for an upright freezer, on top for a chest freezer.

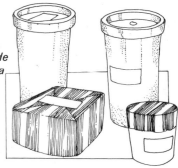

Gingered
125 chocolate cheesecake

You will need . . .

Cooking time
1 hour

Oven setting
180°C, 350°F, Gas Mark 4

Storage time
4–6 months

Defrosting time
2½ hours at room temperature

15 g/½ oz butter
50 g/2 oz semi-sweet biscuits
225 g/8 oz cream cheese
25 g/1 oz plain flour, sifted
75 g/3 oz plain chocolate, melted
2 pieces preserved ginger, chopped
2 eggs
75 g/3 oz castor sugar
When serving:
300 ml/½ pint double cream, whipped
3 pieces preserved ginger, sliced

Use the butter to grease the base and sides of a loose-bottomed 18-cm/7-inch cake tin. Crush the biscuits finely, almost to a powder. Sprinkle over the base and sides of the tin. Smooth a strip of foil around the outside of the tin to protrude slightly above the top edge.

Cream the cheese and the flour together until smooth. Gradually beat in the melted chocolate and chopped ginger. Whisk the eggs and sugar together until light and thick. Add to the chocolate mixture and blend well. Pour into the prepared tin and bake in a moderate oven for 1 hour. Cool in the tin.

To freeze: Open freeze then remove from the tin to a firm base. Cover with a polythene container or bag. Seal and label.
To serve: Unpack and place on a serving dish. Spread the top with whipped cream and pipe a border. Decorate with slices of ginger before defrosting.
Serves 4–6

FREEZING HINT

Always add a little milk to extra thick cream when whipping it for freezing. The high content of butter fat (which separates out if the cream is not whipped) remains in large fat globules, if the cream is too rich or not sufficiently beaten.

Sweet
126 Gouda cheesecake

You will need . . .

Cooking time
60–70 minutes

Oven setting
220°C, 425°F, Gas Mark 7
180°C, 350°F, Gas Mark 4

Storage time
4–6 months

Defrosting time
4 hours at room temperature

225 g/8 oz plain flour
pinch salt
100 g/4 oz butter
2–3 tablespoons water
For the filling:
175 g/6 oz Gouda cheese, grated
2 tablespoons flour
3 tablespoons single cream
finely grated zest and juice of 1 lemon
50 g/2 oz sultanas
2 eggs, separated
75 g/3 oz castor sugar

Place the flour and salt in a bowl, rub in the butter and bind together with the water. Roll out on a floured board to line a 23-cm/9-inch loose-bottomed fluted flan tin. Prick the base with a fork. Bake blind in a hot oven for 15 minutes. Remove and reduce oven heat to moderate.

Meanwhile, mix together the cheese, flour, cream, lemon zest and juice and the sultanas. Whisk the egg yolks and sugar together and add to the cheese mixture, blending well. Whisk the egg whites until stiff and fold in lightly.

Pour the filling into the prepared flan case and bake in a moderate oven for 45–55 minutes. Cool.

To freeze: Open freeze until solid, remove from the tin and pack in a polythene bag. Seal and label.
To serve: Unpack and place on a serving dish to defrost. Sift icing sugar over the top and serve cold with single cream.
Serves 6

FREEZING HINT

Fruit yogurt freezes better than plain yogurt because of the sugar content. Honey stirred into home-made plain yogurt helps to prevent it from separating in the freezer.

Layered
127 cheesecake loaf

A-B-C
128 cherry cheesecake

You will need . . .

Cooking time
about 10 minutes

Storage time
4–6 months

Defrosting time
4 hours at room temperature

2 eggs
4 tablespoons milk
350 g/12 oz cottage cheese, sieved
2 tablespoons flour, sifted
150 g/5 oz sugar
1 teaspoon finely grated orange zest
1 tablespoon orange juice
150 ml/¼ pint double cream, whipped
100 g/4 oz digestive biscuits, crushed
¼ teaspoon ground cinnamon
40 g/1½ oz butter, melted

Beat together the eggs, milk and cheese. Beat in the flour, 75 g/3 oz sugar and the orange zest. Cook in the top of a double boiler or in a basin over simmering water for about 10 minutes, until thickened, stirring. Add the orange juice and cool. Fold in the cream.

Mix together the biscuit crumbs, remaining sugar, cinnamon and melted butter. Line the short sides and base of a 1-kg/2-lb loaf tin with a long strip of double foil, allowing the ends to protrude well above the top of the tin. Cover the base with half the crumbs, spoon over the cheese mixture then the remaining crumbs. Press down lightly.

To freeze: Open freeze until solid then lift out of the tin. Pack in foil or a polythene bag. Seal and label.
To serve: Unpack and place on a serving dish to defrost. Decorate with orange wedges, piped cream and angelica.
Serves 4–6

You will need . . .

Storage time
4–6 months

Defrosting time
2½ hours at room temperature

1 lemon jelly
150 ml/¼ pint boiling water
450 g/1 lb cream cheese
150 ml/5 fl oz natural yogurt
1 (396-g/14-oz) can cherry pie filling
150 ml/¼ pint double cream, whipped
50 g/2 oz butter
100 g/4 oz Nice biscuits, crushed
When serving:
150 ml/¼ pint double cream, whipped

Dissolve the jelly in the boiling water and allow to cool until syrupy. Soften the cream cheese and gradually beat in the yogurt and half the pie filling. Blend in the setting jelly and when well combined fold in the whipped cream.

Lightly oil an 18-cm/7-inch cake tin and line the base with a circle of non-stick or greaseproof paper. Pour in the cherry mixture and chill until firm. Melt the butter and stir in the biscuit crumbs. Sprinkle over the cheese-cake and press with the back of a metal spoon.

Freeze until solid then turn out on to a firm base and remove the paper from the top of the cheesecake. Spread over the remaining pie filling.

To freeze: Open freeze until solid then cover with a polythene container. Seal and label.
To serve: Unpack and place on a serving dish to defrost. Decorate with piped cream.
Serves 6

FREEZING HINT

Margarine and cottage cheese containers are useful for short term storage of items like prepared sandwich fillings, ready to spread on buttered bread when required. The 225 g/8 oz tub holds enough filling to spread eight rounds thinly or six rounds thickly.

FREEZING HINT

When using large catering-size cans of fruit or pie fillings, convenient quantities can be packed and frozen in smaller containers ready for use.

129 Cider sorbet

You will need . . .

Cooking time
15 minutes

Storage time
4–6 months

Defrosting time
30 minutes in the
refrigerator

175 g/6 oz sugar
450 ml/¾ pint water
finely grated zest of 1 lemon
450 ml/¾ pint extra dry still cider
1 egg white
When serving:
1 dessert apple, sliced

Place the sugar, water and lemon zest in a saucepan and stir over gentle heat until the sugar has dissolved. Boil for 10 minutes then allow to cool.

Stir the cider into the syrup and pour into shallow trays. Freeze until firm round the edges. Turn into a chilled bowl and beat until slushy.

Stiffly whisk the egg white and fold into the cider mixture. Return to the trays.

To freeze: Cover trays with foil or repack in a polythene container. Seal and label.
To serve: Keep covered to defrost then scoop into stemmed glasses and decorate with thin slices of dessert apple.
Serves 4

130 Tropical banana ice

You will need . . .

Storage time
4–6 months

Defrosting time
10 minutes at room
temperature

3 ripe bananas
3 tablespoons lemon juice
100 ml/4 fl oz orange juice
6 tablespoons golden syrup
pinch salt
1 egg white
75 g/3 oz castor sugar
250 ml/8 fl oz milk
10 maraschino cherries
3 tablespoons maraschino cherry juice
½ teaspoon grated orange zest

Mash the bananas with the lemon juice. Stir in the orange juice, golden syrup and salt.

Whisk the egg white until frothy, then gradually whisk in the sugar. Fold this into the banana mixture with the milk. Chop the cherries coarsely and stir in with the cherry juice and orange zest.

Pour into shallow containers and freeze for 2 hours. Scoop into a chilled bowl and beat with an electric mixer or hand whisk until light and fluffy.

To freeze: Pack quickly in a polythene container and freeze until firm. Seal and label.
To serve: Allow to soften for 10 minutes at room temperature then scoop into glass dishes. Decorate with sliced glacé cherries and angelica leaves and serve with wafer biscuits, if liked.
Serves 4

FREEZING HINT

A quick party spectacular to freeze. Whisk together a large can of condensed milk, 150 ml/¼ pint double cream, the juice of 3 large lemons and 2 tablespoons sweet sherry. Fold in some grated zest from the lemons and freeze. It tastes gorgeous served chilled.

FREEZING HINT

Use scooped out orange halves as containers for fruit sorbets of any flavour. The juice can be used in the sorbet if required. Fill the orange shells with the sorbet after folding in the egg whites.

131 Gooseberry sherbet

Blackcurrant
132 cheese cream

You will need . . .

450 ml/¾ pint gooseberry purée
1 teaspoon gelatine
½ teaspoon almond essence
green food colouring (optional)
2 egg whites

Cooking time
5–10 minutes

Storage time
12 months

Defrosting time
10 minutes in the
refrigerator

If the fruit purée has been prepared without sieving, it must be sieved to remove all the pips. Heat a few tablespoons of the purée, stir in the gelatine and allow it to dissolve. Add the rest of the purée and the almond essence and stir well. If liked, add a few drops of colouring.

Turn the purée into a bowl, cover the surface lightly with foil and place in the freezer until the mixture has slightly thickened.

Remove, fold in the stiffly beaten egg whites.

To freeze: Divide between polythene containers. Seal and label.
To serve: Transfer to the refrigerator for 10 minutes, then pile into individual glasses.
Serves 4
Note: Large quantities of sherbet are difficult to defrost evenly, therefore it is better to divide this amount between 2 containers.

You will need . . .

15 g/½ oz gelatine
2 tablespoons hot water
50 g/2 oz cottage cheese, sieved
2 tablespoons castor sugar
600 ml/1 pint sweetened blackcurrant
    purée
150 ml/¼ pint double cream
2 egg whites
When serving:
150 ml/¼ pint double cream, whipped

Storage time
4–6 months

Defrosting time
1 hour in the refrigerator

Dissolve the gelatine in the hot water in a basin over a pan of hot water. Combine the cottage cheese and castor sugar in a large bowl, and when smooth whisk in the gelatine and blackcurrant purée gradually. Allow to stand until beginning to set.

Whip the cream lightly and fold into the blackcurrant mixture.

Whisk the egg whites until stiff, fold in, and turn the mixture into a rigid polythene container.

To freeze: Seal and label.
To serve: Remove the polythene container from the freezer, allow to thaw a little and spoon the mixture into individual glass dishes. Smooth the surfaces and decorate with piped whipped cream. Serve chilled. The texture is a little firmer than that of ordinary ice cream.
Serves 4–6

FREEZING HINT

Gooseberries are worth freezing two ways. Pack them raw and whole for fruit pies, or as cooked, sweetened and sieved purée for fools, mousses and sorbets.

FREEZING HINT

No amount of fruit is too small to freeze — make up mixed packs of summer fruits as they become available and use these later for summer puddings, trifles, ice cream desserts or jam making.

133 Chocolate fudge flan

You will need . . .

Cooking time
35–40 minutes

Oven setting
190°C, 375°F, Gas Mark 5

Storage time
4–6 months

Defrosting time
4 hours at room temperature

175 g/6 oz butter
100 g/4 oz digestive biscuits, crushed
100 g/4 oz soft brown sugar
150 g/5 oz self-raising flour
25 g/1 oz cocoa powder
150 ml/¼ pint milk
When serving:
150 ml/¼ pint double cream, whipped

Melt a third of the butter and stir in the biscuit crumbs. Press this mixture firmly to the base and sides of a greased 20-cm/8-inch square shallow cake tin.

Beat together the remaining butter and the sugar until light and fluffy. Add the flour, cocoa and milk and stir until smooth. Spread this mixture over the crumb base.

Bake in a moderately hot oven for 35–40 minutes. Leave to cool in the tin.

To freeze: Open freeze until solid then remove from the tin and pack in a polythene bag. Seal and label.
To serve: Unwrap while frozen, cut into squares and pipe a swirl of cream on each.
Serves 6

FREEZING HINT

Fruits which discolour easily should be defrosted sealed in their wrappings. Avoid exposure to the air as long as possible.

134 Grapefruit chiffon pie

You will need . . .

Cooking time
10 minutes

Oven setting
180°C, 350°F, Gas Mark 4

Storage time
4–6 months

Defrosting time
8 hours in the refrigerator or 3 hours at room temperature

50 g/2 oz butter
25 g/1 oz castor sugar
75 g/3 oz desiccated coconut
7 g/¼ oz gelatine
300 ml/½ pint unsweetened grapefruit juice
175 g/6 oz granulated sugar
½ teaspoon salt
2 eggs, separated
2 tablespoons lemon juice
150 ml/¼ pint double cream, whipped
grapefruit segments for decoration

Melt the butter and stir in the sugar and coconut. Pat evenly over the sides and base of a 20-cm/8-inch foil flan case. Bake in a moderate oven for 6 minutes. Cool.

Meanwhile, make the filling. Soften the gelatine in the grapefruit juice, then dissolve over a low heat. Stir in the sugar and salt. Add the egg yolks and cook over medium heat for 1 minute, stirring constantly. Add the lemon juice and chill until the mixture is on the point of setting.

Whisk the egg whites until stiff and fold into the setting mixture, then fold in half the cream. Spoon into the prepared coconut crust. Allow to set. Decorate with the remaining cream and the grapefruit segments.

To freeze: Open freeze until solid, cover with foil. Seal and label.
To serve: Unwrap while frozen and defrost.
Serves 4–6

FREEZING HINT

When only the juice of citrus fruit is required for a recipe, freeze the grated zest mixed with a little sugar. It is a useful standby for flavouring cakes and desserts.

135 Parfait cream pie

You will need . . .

Storage time
4–6 months

Defrosting time
30 minutes in the refrigerator

1 (69-g/2.4-oz) packet strawberry
    Angel Delight
150 ml/¼ pint single cream
150 ml/¼ pint cold milk
2 tablespoons cherry brandy
4 tablespoons drained Maraschino
    cherries
2 large coconut macaroons, crumbled
When serving:
150 ml/¼ pint double cream, whipped
Maraschino cherries, drained

Use a strip of foil to line the base and short sides of a 450-g/
1-lb loaf tin, leaving the ends of the strip protruding above
the edges of the tin.

Make up the Angel Delight using the cream and milk
and stir in the cherry brandy.

Pour half this mixture into the prepared tin. Sprinkle
over the cherries and macaroon crumbs and top with the
remainder of the creamy mixture. Smooth the top and
allow to set.

To freeze: Open freeze until solid then lift out of the tin
using the foil strip and pack in foil or a polythene bag. Seal
and label.
To serve: Unwrap while frozen and place on a serving
dish to defrost. Spread over whipped cream and decorate
with piped cream and Maraschino cherries. Serve sliced
while chilled but not frozen.
Serves 4–6

FREEZING HINT

*Cover custard to be frozen with a
good layer of demerara sugar. It
melts to form a caramel topping
as the custard defrosts and
disguises the tendency to separate.*

136 Banana ice cream pie

You will need . . .

Cooking time
5 minutes

Storage time
4–6 months

Defrosting time
20 minutes in the refrigerator

75 g/3 oz butter
3 tablespoons golden syrup
3 tablespoons cocoa powder
100 g/4 oz cornflakes
2 bananas, sliced
about 1 litre/35 fl oz vanilla ice cream
When serving:
50 g/2 oz plain chocolate, grated

Place the butter, syrup and cocoa in a saucepan and heat
gently, stirring until smooth. Remove from the heat and
stir in the cornflakes.

Press this mixture into the base and sides of a 20-cm/
8-inch foil flan case and chill well.

Arrange the banana slices in the bottom of the prepared
flan case and cover completely with neat scoops of firm
ice cream.

To freeze: Open freeze until solid then cover with lid or
foil. Seal and label.
To serve: Uncover to defrost, sprinkle with grated
chocolate and cut into wedges. For parties, pour over hot
Chocolate marshmallow sauce (see recipe 214).
Serves 4–6

FREEZING HINT

*To vary this dessert – use a
different fruit and a complementary
ice cream. Try mandarin oranges
with chocolate ice cream, or fresh
raspberries with raspberry ripple
ice cream.*

Coffee nut-and-
137 fruit ice cream

You will need . . .

1 tablespoon instant coffee powder
4 tablespoons boiling water
2 eggs

Storage time
6 months

100 g/4 oz icing sugar, sifted
300 ml/½ pint double cream

Defrosting time
1 hour in the refrigerator

50 g/2 oz walnut halves, finely chopped
50 g/2 oz seedless raisins, chopped

Dissolve the coffee powder in the boiling water and allow to cool. Separate the eggs and whisk the whites until stiff. Fold in the sifted icing sugar.

Whisk the egg yolks and coffee mixture together in a large bowl. Fold in the whisked egg white mixture and combine thoroughly. Half whip the cream, so that it just begins to hold traces of the beaters, then fold into the mixture in the bowl, with the chopped walnut halves and raisins.

To freeze: Pour into freezing trays or a polythene container. (This ice cream needs no further beating when partly frozen.) Seal and label.

To serve: Transfer to the refrigerator and allow to soften until the ice cream can easily be scooped out. As it is very rich, serve with plain vanilla wafer biscuits.
Serves 4–6

Rippled
138 apricot ice cream

You will need . . .

75 g/3 oz sugar
150 ml/¼ pint water
450 g/1 lb apricots

Cooking time
10–15 minutes

150 ml/¼ pint double cream
6 tablespoons apricot jam

Storage time
4–6 months

Defrosting time
30 minutes in the
refrigerator

Place the sugar and water in a saucepan and bring to the boil. Halve and stone the apricots, add to the sugar syrup and poach gently for about 10 minutes. Blend in a liquidiser or press through a sieve and allow to cool completely.

Whip the cream and fold into the apricot mixture. Place in a shallow container and freeze until firm.

Warm the apricot jam then sieve. Turn the frozen mixture into a bowl and beat until smooth. Gently fold in the sieved jam to give a rippled effect.

To freeze: Pack in a shallow foil or polythene container. Seal and label.

To serve: Soften in the refrigerator while still sealed in the pack. Serve scooped into individual dishes.
Serves 4

FREEZING HINT

If you can buy coffee more cheaply in larger quantities, remember that freshly roasted coffee beans freeze for up to 1 year, while repacked instant coffee freezes for 3 months.

FREEZING HINT

Instant sweets from the freezer are much in demand. Try mixing 300 ml/½ pint sieved and sweetened gooseberry purée with an equal quantity of canned custard or soft vanilla ice cream. Freeze in individual portions.

139 Pineapple prune freeze

Raspberry
140 ratafia ice cream

You will need . . .

1 (425-g/15-oz) can prunes
2 egg whites
225 g/8 oz castor sugar
1 (376-g/13¼-oz) can crushed pineapple
½ (178-ml/6¼-fl oz) can frozen
    unsweetened orange juice concentrate,
    defrosted
300 ml/½ pint double cream

Storage time
4–6 months

Defrosting time
30 minutes in the
refrigerator

Stone the prunes then liquidise with the syrup from the can or press the contents through a sieve, to make a purée.

Whisk the egg whites until stiff then sprinkle in half the sugar and continue whisking until the mixture is glossy and stands in firm peaks. Fold in the remaining sugar then the purée, the crushed pineapple and syrup from the can and the orange juice.

Whip the cream until thick and fold lightly into the fruit mixture until well blended.

To freeze: Pack in shallow foil or polythene containers. Seal and label.
To serve: Soften in the refrigerator while still sealed in the pack. Scoop into individual dishes and serve.
Serves 6–8

You will need . . .

300 ml/½ pint milk
2 eggs, separated
75 g/3 oz castor sugar
½ teaspoon almond essence
300 ml/½ pint raspberry purée
450 ml/¾ pint double cream
75 g/3 oz ratafia biscuits
    or macaroons, crumbled

Cooking time
15 minutes

Storage time
4–6 months

Defrosting time
30 minutes in the refrigerator

Put the milk, egg yolks, sugar and almond essence in a bowl over a pan of hot water. Cook, stirring occasionally, until the custard thickens sufficiently to coat the back of a spoon. Remove bowl from the heat and leave the custard to cool.

When cold, stir in the fruit purée. Whip the cream until it forms soft peaks and stir into the mixture. Gently fold in the crumbled ratafia biscuits or macaroons. Lastly, fold in the stiffly whisked egg whites.

Cover the bowl lightly with foil and place in the freezer until partially frozen. Remove, beat the mixture until smooth.

To freeze: Divide between polythene containers. Seal and label.
To serve: Transfer to the refrigerator for 30 minutes, then spoon into individual dishes.
Serves 4–6

FREEZING HINT

When you want to serve a festive sweet suddenly, but have only vanilla ice cream in the freezer, here is a quick way to produce a dreamy sauce. Melt two Mars Bars with four tablespoons of milk in a basin over hot water, and pour over scoops of ice cream.

FREEZING HINT

Berries such as strawberries and raspberries combine well with less exotic partners like rhubarb and apple. The flavour of the berries seems to predominate.

Gorgeous gâteaux

When you have tried my recipes for everyday cakes and cookies you will know how easy it is to produce mouth-watering teatime treats which taste as good as they look. The fabulous gâteaux in this section may appear elaborate but take little more time and trouble to achieve. Study the decorations in the colour photographs. Florentine cake, for instance, is simply coated with melted chocolate and marked with a fork, while Date and pineapple gâteau is really an upside-down cake turned out and finished with a glaze. If you don't have the time to pipe decorations, a very pretty effect can be achieved by simply spreading and swirling cream.

141 Ginger meringue cake

(illustrated on frontispiece)

You will need . . .

Cooking time
2½–3 hours

Oven setting
110°C, 225°F, Gas Mark ¼

Storage time
3–4 months

Defrosting time
3 hours at room temperature

4 egg whites
175 g/6 oz soft brown sugar
50 g/2 oz castor sugar
For the filling:
300 ml/½ pint whipping cream
1 tablespoon ginger syrup
2 tablespoons chopped stem ginger
2 tablespoons chopped hazelnuts
few slices stem ginger

Line 3 baking trays with foil, or use non-stick baking trays. Mark 3 circles, each 18 cm/7 inches in diameter.
   Whisk the egg whites until firm and glossy, gradually whisk in the brown sugar then fold in the castor sugar. Spread over the 3 marked circles. Bake in the coolest oven for 2½–3 hours, until quite dry. Peel away the foil. Cool the meringues on a wire tray. Whip the cream. Reserve some for decoration then whip the ginger syrup into the remainder and fold in the chopped ginger and hazelnuts. Use to sandwich the meringue layers, on a serving plate. Pipe a border of cream and decorate with stem ginger.

To freeze: Put the plate on a large square of foil and open freeze the cake. When hard, fold in the corners and seal.
To serve: Thaw uncovered, removing the foil.

FREEZING HINT

After open freezing a decorated gâteau, you can pack it carefully in a polythene bag. Draw out excess air with an air pump and seal with a twist tie, being careful not to damage the decorations.

Strawberry 142 and orange meringue

You will need . . .

Cooking time
2–2½ hours

Oven setting
110°C, 225°F, Gas Mark ¼

Storage time
3–4 months

Defrosting time
3 hours at room temperature

2 egg whites
pinch salt
pinch cream of tartar
100 g/4 oz castor sugar
For the filling:
1 large orange
1 (69-g/2.4-oz) packet strawberry Angel Delight
150 ml/¼ pint cold milk
150 ml/¼ pint single cream

Whisk the egg whites with the salt and cream of tartar until stiff. Gradually whisk in half the sugar and continue whisking until the mixture stands in glossy peaks. Fold in the remaining sugar.
   Pipe half the meringue mixture into a 20-cm/8-inch circle on a baking tray lined with non-stick paper. Fit a star tube to the piping bag, fill with the remaining mixture and pipe a good edge of rosettes to the meringue circle. Bake in a very cool oven for 2–2½ hours, until quite dry. Cool.
   Meanwhile, grate the orange zest and divide the flesh into segments. Make up the Angel Delight with the milk and cream. Fold in the orange zest and segments, pour into the meringue case and place on a serving plate.

To freeze: Open freeze until solid then pack in a polythene container for protection. Seal and label.
To serve: Uncover while still frozen. Decorate with a few whole strawberries, if liked.

FREEZING HINT

Icing which has been frozen prepared in a bag may not beat smooth when defrosted. If possible freeze in a boiling bag and place in hot water for 10 minutes before turning out.

Pineapple
143 macaroon layer gâteau

You will need . . .

Cooking time
25 minutes

Oven setting
160°C, 325°F, Gas Mark 3

Storage time
3–4 months

Defrosting time
4 hours at room temperature

4 egg whites
225 g/8 oz castor sugar
50g/2 oz ground almonds
few drops almond essence
For the filling:
75 g/3 oz butter
175 g/6 oz icing sugar
1 teaspoon finely grated lemon zest
1 egg yolk
175 g/6 oz drained canned pineapple
  pieces
150 ml/¼ pint double cream, whipped

Whisk the egg whites until stiff. Add half the castor sugar and whisk again until stiff. Fold in the remaining castor sugar, the ground almonds and the almond essence. Grease and flour three baking trays or line them with non-stick paper. Draw a 20-cm/8-inch circle on each tray and pipe on the macaroon mixture. Bake in a moderate oven for 25 minutes. Cool on the trays then carefully remove with a palette knife.

Meanwhile, cream the butter and beat in the icing sugar, lemon zest and egg yolk. Finely chop half the pineapple pieces and add to the filling mixture.

Sandwich the macaroon layers together with the pine-apple cream. Pipe a border of whipped cream around the edge of the cake and decorate with the remaining pine-apple pieces. Place the cake on a serving plate.

To freeze: Open freeze until firm then pack in a polythene container. Seal and label.
To serve: Uncover while still frozen.

FREEZING HINT

Frozen fruit to be eaten raw should be served while still chilled in the centre otherwise the texture tends to be a little flabby.

Mincemeat
144 cream angel cake

You will need . . .

Cooking time
1 hour

Oven setting
180°C, 350°F, Gas Mark 4

Storage time
4–6 months

Defrosting time
8 hours in the refrigerator

100 g/4 oz plain flour
185 g/6½ oz castor sugar
6 egg whites
½ teaspoon cream of tartar
½ teaspoon vanilla essence
few drops almond essence
300 ml/½ pint double cream
225 g/8 oz mincemeat
25 g/1 oz icing sugar, sifted
25 g/1 oz long stranded coconut,
  toasted

Sift the flour and almost half the sugar together three times. Whisk the egg whites and cream of tartar until frothy. Gradually add the remaining sugar, whisking until the mixture stands in glossy peaks. Add the essences then fold in the sifted flour and sugar.

Turn into an ungreased 20-cm/8-inch ring tin and draw a knife through the mixture several times to release any air bubbles. Bake in a moderate oven for 1 hour. Invert the tin over a cake rack and leave until the cake is cold – it will then fall out whole.

Whip the cream until thick and fold the mincemeat into half of it. Cut the cake into three layers and sandwich together with the mincemeat cream. Add the icing sugar to the remaining cream and spread over the cake. Sprinkle with the coconut and place on a serving plate.

To freeze: Open freeze until solid, then pack in a poly-thene container. Seal and label.
To serve: Uncover and defrost but serve cold.

FREEZING HINT

Egg yolks freeze well and should be stirred lightly before the addition of ½ teaspoon salt or ¾ teaspoon sugar to each 5 yolks. Pack leaving a headspace, labelled for savoury or sweet use.

145 Citrus fudge cake

You will need . . .

Cooking time
40–45 minutes

Oven setting
190°C, 375°F, Gas Mark 5

Storage time
4–6 months

Defrosting time
4 hours at room temperature

275 g/10 oz butter
175 g/6 oz castor sugar
juice and zest of 1 orange
juice and zest of 1 lemon
3 eggs
175 g/6 oz self-raising flour
pinch salt
3 tablespoons golden syrup
175 g/6 oz icing sugar
75 g/3 oz nuts, chopped
crystallised orange and lemon slices

Cream 175 g/6 oz butter with the castor sugar until light and fluffy. Add the grated fruit zests and the eggs, one at a time, beating well. Sift the flour with the salt and fold into the mixture with 2 tablespoons orange juice.

Turn into a greased and lined loose-bottomed 23-cm/ 9-inch cake tin and bake in a moderately hot oven for 40–45 minutes, until pale golden and firm to the touch. Turn out on a wire tray and strip off the lining paper. Cool.

Meanwhile, melt the remaining butter with the golden syrup and 2 tablespoons lemon juice. Beat in the icing sugar until smooth. Chill well then spread the sides of the cake with a little of this frosting and roll in the chopped nuts. Place on a serving plate, top with the remaining frosting, using a palette knife. Decorate with orange and lemon slices.

To freeze: Open freeze until firm then pack in a polythene container. Seal and label.
To serve: Unpack while still frozen.

FREEZING HINT

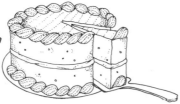

When defrosting a large cake with soft icing on the outside, it will be easier to cut into wedges if sliced before fully defrosted.

146 Orange finger cake

You will need . . .

Storage time
4–6 months

Defrosting time
4 hours at room temperature

100 g/4 oz butter
150 g/5 oz castor sugar
4 egg yolks
grated zest of 1 orange
1 teaspoon lemon juice
2 tablespoons orange juice
about 30 sponge fingers
1 (312-g/11-oz) can mandarin oranges
When serving:
4 tablespoons double cream, whipped
few mandarin orange segments

Use a strip of foil to line the base and short sides of a 1-kg/2-lb loaf tin, leaving the ends of the strip to protrude above the edges of the tin.

Cream the butter with the sugar until light and fluffy. Gradually beat in the egg yolks and then the orange zest and fruit juices. Reserve 8 sponge fingers, then use the remainder to line the base and long sides of the prepared tin, dipping them first in the syrup drained from the mandarins. Spoon in half the orange mixture, cover with the drained mandarins and spoon over the remaining mixture. Trim the biscuits to the level of the filling and press the trimmings lightly into the top of the orange mixture. Lay over the reserved sponge fingers.

Allow to stand at room temperature for 2 hours.

To freeze: Open freeze until solid, then lift out of the tin and pack in foil. Seal and label.
To serve: Unwrap while frozen and place on a serving dish to defrost. Decorate with piped cream and mandarins

FREEZING HINT

To use frozen eggs, whether whole or separated, remember that 2 tablespoons of whole egg mixture equals 1 fresh egg. If separated for freezing, 1 tablespoon of white and 1 tablespoon of yolk combined equals 1 whole egg.

Lemon
147 chiffon charlotte

You will need . . .

Storage time
4–6 months

Defrosting time
5 hours in the refrigerator

1 lemon jelly
150 ml/¼ pint boiling water
1 orange
2 tablespoons sweet sherry
16 sponge fingers
1 (44-g/1½-oz) sachet dessert topping
  mix
150 ml/¼ pint cold milk
1 (425-g/15-oz) can custard
When serving:
150 ml/¼ pint double cream, whipped
1 slice orange

Dissolve the jelly in the boiling water and allow to stand until syrupy.

Meanwhile, finely grate the zest from the orange and squeeze the juice. Mix the orange juice with the sherry. Dip the fingers into the sherry mixture and use to line the dimples of a Tupperware Jel 'N Serve.

Make up the topping mix with the cold milk. Blend the custard and orange zest into the setting jelly, then fold in the topping mix. Spoon this mixture into the centre of the lined mould. Put on the seal and allow to stand at room temperature for 2 hours.

To freeze: Check the seals and label.
To serve: Remove the large seal while the charlotte is still frozen, invert the mould over a serving plate and remove the top seal. Leave for a few minutes to allow the charlotte to drop out of the mould, then defrost. Decorate with piped rosettes of cream and a twisted orange slice.
Note: Canned custard is much more satisfactory for freezing than home-made custard.

FREEZING HINT

Both orange and lemon curds are delicious, but will keep for only a short time in a cupboard. Frozen in small jars or containers, storage time will be 12 months.

Coffee
148 and hazelnut roulade

You will need . . .

Cooking time
15 minutes

Oven setting
190°C, 375°F, Gas Mark 5

Storage time
4–6 months

Defrosting time
4 hours at room temperature

3 eggs
75 g/3 oz castor sugar
25 g/1 oz ground hazelnuts
50 g/2 oz self-raising flour
1 tablespoon coffee essence
castor sugar for sprinkling
For the buttercream:
100 g/4 oz butter
175 g/6 oz icing sugar
50 g/2 oz ground hazelnuts
1 egg white
few whole hazelnuts

Whisk the eggs and sugar until thick and creamy. Fold in the hazelnuts, flour and coffee essence and spread in a greased and lined Swiss roll tin. Bake in a moderately hot oven for 15 minutes, until pale golden and firm to the touch. Turn out on a sheet of sugared greaseproof paper and strip off the lining paper. Roll up loosely with the sugared paper inside and cool.

Meanwhile, make the buttercream. Cream the butter, add the icing sugar, ground hazelnuts and egg white and beat until smooth and light.

Carefully unroll the hazelnut sponge and spread with buttercream. Roll up, coat with the remaining buttercream and pipe a line of rosettes down the centre. Decorate with the whole hazelnuts and place on a serving plate.

To freeze: Open freeze until firm then pack in a polythene container. Seal and label.
To serve: Unpack while still frozen.

FREEZING HINT

Make a chocolate Swiss roll sponge and cool rolled up with a clean tea towel. Unroll and fill with softened vanilla ice cream. Roll and seal tightly in foil to freeze.

149 Rum and banana cake

You will need . . .	2 bananas
	4 tablespoons soured cream
Cooking time	4 tablespoons rum
about 50 minutes	3 eggs
	75 g/3 oz castor sugar
Oven setting	275 g/10 oz plain flour, sifted
200°C, 400°F, Gas Mark 6	50 g/2 oz butter, melted
	150 ml/¼ pint water
Storage time	4 teaspoons lemon juice
4–6 months	100 g/4 oz granulated sugar
	When serving:
Defrosting time	150 ml/¼ pint double cream, whipped
4 hours at room temperature	few slices banana

Mash the bananas with the soured cream and half the rum. Whisk the eggs and castor sugar together until thick and creamy. Fold in the flour, melted butter, and the banana mixture. Pour into a greased 23-cm/9-inch ring tin and bake in a moderately hot oven for 40–45 minutes, until risen and firm to the touch.

Meanwhile, put the water, lemon juice and granulated sugar into a saucepan and stir until the sugar dissolves. Bring to the boil and simmer for 10 minutes. Stir in the remaining rum.

Turn out the baked cake and place on a serving plate. Prick all over with a fine skewer while still warm and spoon over the rum syrup. Cool.

To freeze: Open freeze until solid then pack in a polythene container. Seal and label.
To serve: Uncover while still frozen and decorate with whipped cream and banana slices immediately before serving.

FREEZING HINT

When soaking a cake with syrup of any kind before freezing, seal, chill for an hour, then invert the pack before placing in the freezer. This helps to distribute the syrup.

150 Apricot rum gâteau

You will need . . .	175 g/6 oz butter, softened
	175 g/6 oz castor sugar
	3 eggs
Cooking time	175 g/6 oz self-raising flour
35–45 minutes	*For the syrup:*
	1 (425-g/15-oz) can apricot halves
Oven setting	100 g/4 oz granulated sugar
190°C, 375°F, Gas Mark 5	2 teaspoons instant coffee powder
	2 tablespoons rum
Storage time	*To decorate:*
4–6 months	150 ml/¼ pint whipping cream
Defrosting time	drained apricot halves
8 hours in the refrigerator or	angelica leaves
4 hours at room temperature	

Put the butter into a warm mixing bowl with the sugar, eggs and flour. Beat for 1–2 minutes until well blended. Turn into a greased 20-cm/8-inch cake tin. Bake in a moderately hot oven for 35–45 minutes.

Meanwhile, make up the rum syrup. Drain the apricots. Dissolve the sugar in the syrup from the can over gentle heat. Simmer for 2 minutes, then stir in the coffee powder and the rum. Turn the baked cake on to a large plate and spoon over the syrup. Allow to soak in. Cool.

To decorate, whip the cream until stiff. Place the cake on a serving plate and pipe a shell border of cream round the edge. Fill the centre with the drained apricot halves and decorate with the remaining cream and the angelica.

To freeze: Put the cake complete on its serving plate on a large square of foil and open freeze on a baking tray. When hard, fold in the corners and seal completely. Label.
To serve: Thaw uncovered, removing the plate from the sheet of foil.

FREEZING HINT

Victoria sandwich cake mixture can be frozen uncooked. Measure out in lidded plastic bowls, or containers, to make layers of similar size.

151 Chocolate cherry cake

You will need . . .

Cooking time
25–35 minutes

Oven setting
160°C, 325°F, Gas Mark 3

Storage time
4–6 months

Defrosting time
4 hours at room temperature

100 g/4 oz self-raising flour
2 tablespoons cocoa powder
1 teaspoon baking powder
100 g/4 oz soft margarine
100 g/4 oz castor sugar
2 eggs
For the filling:
2 (44-g/1½-oz) sachets dessert topping mix
300 ml/½ pint cold milk
1 tablespoon Kirsch
1 (396-g/14-oz) can cherry pie filling

Sift the flour, cocoa and baking powder together into a bowl and add the margarine, sugar and eggs. Beat well for 2–3 minutes, until smooth.

Divide between two greased and base-lined 18-cm/7-inch sandwich tins and bake in a moderate oven for 25–35 minutes. Turn out the cakes and cool on a wire tray.

Place one cake on a serving plate or firm base. Make up the topping mixes with the cold milk and use half to cover the cake base. Top with the second cake. Stir the Kirsch into the pie filling. Pipe the remaining topping mix around the top of the cake and fill the centre with the pie filling.

To freeze: Open freeze until solid then cover with a polythene container. Seal and label.
To serve: Unpack while still frozen hard to avoid damage.

FREEZING HINT

Open freeze all decorated cakes before freezing then place in a rigid container if possible.

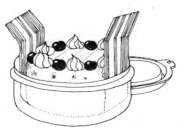

Date and 152 pineapple gâteau

You will need . . .

Cooking time
45 minutes

Oven setting
190°C, 375°F, Gas Mark 5

Storage time
4–6 months

Defrosting time
4 hours at room temperature

200 g/7 oz butter
8 or 9 canned pineapple rings
8 or 9 glacé cherries
175 g/6 oz castor sugar
3 eggs, beaten
175 g/6 oz self-raising flour
pinch salt
½ teaspoon ground mixed spice
75 g/3 oz stoned fresh dates, chopped
6 tablespoons apricot jam

Grease and line a deep 20-cm/8-inch cake tin and grease the lining generously with 25 g/1 oz of the butter. Arrange the pineapple rings on the base and around the sides of the tin. Fill the centre of each ring with a cherry.

Cream the remaining butter with the sugar until light and fluffy. Add the eggs, one at a time, beating well into the mixture. Sift the flour with the salt and spice and fold into the creamed mixture with the chopped dates. Pour into the prepared tin and bake in a moderately hot oven for 45 minutes.

Turn the cake out carefully on to a wire tray. Melt the jam, sieve it and use to brush the cake all over while still warm. Cool and place on a serving plate.

To freeze: Open freeze until solid then pack in a polythene container. Seal and label.
To serve: Uncover while still frozen.

FREEZING HINT

Fruit loses 25% of its pectin content on freezing so remember to freeze down extra fruit for jam making later in the year.

153 Chocolate potato cake

You will need . . .

Cooking time
35–40 minutes

Oven setting
180°C, 350°F, Gas Mark 4

Storage time
4–6 months

Defrosting time
4 hours at room temperature

100 g/4 oz butter
400 g/14 oz castor sugar
3 eggs
175 g/6 oz hot mashed potato
1 teaspoon vanilla essence
200 g/7 oz plain flour
2½ teaspoons baking powder
40 g/1½ oz cocoa powder
75 g/3 oz cream cheese
50 g/2 oz plain chocolate, melted
350 g/12 oz icing sugar, sifted
1 tablespoon milk
chocolate vermicelli
grated chocolate

Cream the butter and sugar until light and pale in colour. Beat in the eggs, one at a time, then add the potato and vanilla essence. Sift the flour, baking powder and cocoa and beat into the mixture. Divide between two greased and base-lined 20-cm/8-inch sandwich tins and bake in a moderate oven for 35–40 minutes, until firm to the touch. Cool in the tins for 5 minutes then turn out on a wire tray.

Beat together the cream cheese and melted chocolate and gradually work in the icing sugar and milk. Sandwich the cooled cakes together with some of the icing and swirl the remainder over the top and sides. Roll the sides of the cake in chocolate vermicelli and decorate the top with grated chocolate and a dusting of icing sugar.

To freeze: Open freeze until solid then pack in a polythene bag. Seal and label.
To serve: Unpack while still frozen and defrost.

FREEZING HINT

When making a layer cake, double the quantities and freeze the extra layers for future use.

154 Florentine cake

You will need . . .

Cooking time
about 1¾ hours

Oven setting
150°C, 300°F, Gas Mark 2

Storage time
4–6 months

Defrosting time
4 hours at room temperature

175 g/6 oz margarine
200 g/7 oz black treacle
75 g/3 oz golden syrup
150 ml/¼ pint soured cream
3 eggs
350 g/12 oz self-raising flour
1½ teaspoons ground mixed spice
3 teaspoons ground ginger
75 g/3 oz soft brown sugar
75 g/3 oz nuts, chopped
75 g/3 oz chopped mixed peel
50 g/2 oz glacé cherries, chopped
175 g/6 oz plain chocolate

Melt the margarine, treacle and golden syrup in a saucepan. Add the soured cream and cool slightly. Beat in the eggs. Sift the flour and spices into a bowl and stir in the brown sugar, nuts, mixed peel and cherries. Add the syrup mixture and beat until smooth. Pour into a greased and lined loose-bottomed 23-cm/9-inch cake tin and bake in a cool oven for 1½–1¾ hours, until firm to the touch. Turn out on a wire tray, strip off the lining paper and cool.

Melt the chocolate, pour over the cake to coat the top and sides, and when on the point of setting, make zig-zag grooves with the back of a fork. Cool.

To freeze: Open freeze until firm then pack in a polythene container. Seal and label.
To serve: Unwrap while still frozen and place on a serving dish to defrost.

FREEZING HINT

If a large rich cake might be wasted when defrosted, consider making in a loaf shape, slicing with dividers and removing only the number of slices required. Or cut in wedges with dividers and reassemble into a circle.

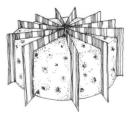

Candy-sweet
155 coffee cake

Chestnut
156 and chocolate gâteau

You will need . . .

Cooking time
about 30 minutes

Oven setting
190°C, 375°F, Gas Mark 5

Storage time
4–6 months

Defrosting time
4 hours at room temperature

225 g/8 oz self-raising flour
100 g/4 oz castor sugar
100 g/4 oz soft margarine
1 tablespoon instant coffee powder
225 g/8 oz golden syrup
2 eggs
4 tablespoons milk
For the coffee cream:
300 ml/½ pint double cream
2 teaspoons golden syrup
1 tablespoon coffee essence
When serving:
chocolate curls

Sift the flour into a bowl. Heat together the sugar, margarine, coffee powder and syrup until melted then allow to become lukewarm. Mix the eggs and milk, add to the flour with the syrup mixture and beat until smooth.

Divide between two greased and base-lined 20-cm/8-inch sandwich tins and bake in a moderately hot oven for 25 minutes. Cool in the tins for 5 minutes then turn out on a wire tray.

Whip the cream and gradually add the syrup and coffee essence. When the cakes are cold, sandwich them together with a little of the coffee cream. Place on a rigid base and spread coffee cream over the top and sides. Use the remaining coffee cream to pipe a border around the base.

To freeze: Open freeze on the rigid base. When solid, cover with a polythene container. Seal and label.
To serve: Uncover while still frozen and decorate with chocolate curls before serving.

You will need . . .

Cooking time
25–30 minutes

Oven setting
180°C, 350°F, Gas Mark 4

Storage time
4–6 months

Defrosting time
4 hours at room temperature

6 eggs
175 g/6 oz castor sugar
125 g/4½ oz self-raising flour
40 g/1½ oz cocoa powder
3 tablespoons oil
3 tablespoons Maraschino
300 ml/½ pint sweetened chestnut purée
75 g/3 oz toasted flaked almonds
Maraschino cherries and angelica
    stalks, or marrons glacés

Whisk the eggs and sugar together until thick and creamy and the whisk leaves a trail when lifted from the mixture. Sift the flour and cocoa together and fold into the whisked mixture with the oil.

Divide evenly between three greased and lined 20-cm/8-inch sandwich tins and bake in a moderate oven for 25–30 minutes, until firm to the touch. Turn out on a wire rack, strip off the lining paper and prick the cakes all over with a fine skewer. Sprinkle with the Maraschino and cool.

Sandwich the cakes together with a little chestnut purée. Spread the remaining purée over the sides and top of the cake then cover all over with toasted almonds. Place on a serving plate and decorate with Maraschino cherries filled with angelica stalks, or quartered marrons glacés.

To freeze: Open freeze until firm then pack in a polythene container. Seal and label.
To serve: Uncover while still frozen.

FREEZING HINT

To make iced coffee quickly take frozen cubes made with double-strength black coffee, sweetened to taste. Mix in the glass with cold milk and add a scoop of vanilla ice cream or whipped cream.

FREEZING HINT

Cakes or gâteaux to be soaked with syrup before freezing should not be allowed to get cold. Pour the syrup over the warm cake. If the cake is cooled, wrap loosely in foil and warm in the oven.

Beautiful breads

Baking your own bread represents a real saving, even allowing for the cost of fuel. Whether you use a packet of bread mix or start from scratch with your own bubbling yeast mixture, the aroma of fresh baked bread is a promise of real delights to come. Fancy rolls which cost so much to buy are really very simple to make, and you can bake loaves in just the shape and size your family requires, for slicing and spreading, toasting and sandwich making.

My section on bread-making extends the gamut to all sorts of scones, sweet and savoury, cooked in the oven or in a heavy frying pan which takes the place of the traditional girdle, plus some exciting new ideas for muffins and teabreads.

158 White bread mix rolls

157 White bread mix loaves

(illustrated on back of jacket)

You will need . . .
1 (850-g/1 lb 14-oz) pack white bread mix
625 ml/generous 1 pint hot water
¼ teaspoon caraway seeds

Cooking time
25–30 minutes

Oven setting
230°C, 450°F, Gas Mark 8

Storage time
6 weeks

Defrosting time
3 hours at room temperature

Place the bread mix in a large bowl and add the hot water. This should be as hot as the hand can stand. Beat with a wooden spoon or by hand until the water is absorbed. Turn out on a floured surface and knead for at least 5 minutes.

Divide into 3 portions and shape into plaited loaves: divide each portion into three and form each piece into a roll about 25 cm/10 inches long. Place the 3 rolls together and plait them from the centre. Place the 3 shaped loaves on greased baking sheets, cover with greased polythene and allow to rise until doubled. Sprinkle with caraway seeds and bake in a hot oven for 25–30 minutes. Cool.

To freeze: Pack in foil or a polythene bag. Seal and label.
To serve: Defrost in the sealed pack.
Makes 3 loaves

FREEZING HINT

Sliced bread can be toasted immediately from the frozen state as the slices separate easily and can be placed straight in the toaster or under the grill.

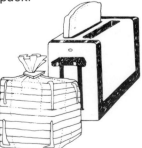

You will need . . .
1 (850-g/1 lb 14-oz) pack white bread mix
100 g/4 oz butter
625 ml/generous 1 pint hot water

Cooking time
about 15 minutes

Oven setting
220°C, 425°F, Gas Mark 7

Storage time
6 weeks

Defrosting time
3 hours at room temperature

Place the bread mix in a large bowl and rub in 75 g/3 oz of the butter. Add the hot water. This should be as hot as the hand can stand. Beat with a wooden spoon or by hand until the water is absorbed. Turn out on a floured surface and knead for at least 5 minutes.

Divide into 4 equal portions. Roll each portion to a circle about 25 cm/10 inches in diameter. Melt the remaining butter and use to brush the circles. Cut each circle into 8 wedge-shaped pieces. Roll up each piece from the wide end to the pointed end and place on a greased baking sheet with the point underneath. Curve the rolls to form crescent shapes. Brush with the remaining melted butter.

Cover with greased polythene and allow to rise until double in size. Bake in a hot oven for 15 minutes. Cool.

To freeze: Pack in a polythene bag. Seal and label.
To serve: Defrost in the sealed pack.
Makes 32

FREEZING HINT

Some people never succeed in making a completely airtight seal with a twist tie. Exceptional strength is not needed; fold the tie around the neck of the bag twice, bring the ends together and twist them three or four times to make the seal really tight.

Brown
159 bread mix loaves

160 Brown bread mix rolls

You will need . . .

1 (850-g/1 lb 14-oz) pack brown bread mix
625 ml/generous 1 pint hot water
15 g/½ oz butter, melted
½ teaspoon yeast extract spread

Cooking time
25–30 minutes

Oven setting
230°C, 450°F, Gas Mark 8

Storage time
6 weeks

Defrosting time
3 hours at room temperature

Place the bread mix in a large bowl and add the hot water. This should be as hot as the hand can stand. Beat with a wooden spoon or by hand until the water is absorbed. Turn out on a floured surface and knead for at least 5 minutes.

Divide into 3 equal portions. Divide each portion in half and shape each piece to a rope about 30 cm/12 inches long. Twist the two ropes together and tuck the ends under to neaten. Mix together the melted butter and yeast extract spread and sprinkle over the twists.

Place the shaped loaves on greased baking sheets, cover with greased polythene and allow to rise until double in size. Bake in a hot oven for 25–30 minutes. Cool.

To freeze: Pack in foil or polythene bags. Seal and label.
To serve: Defrost in the sealed pack.
Makes 3 loaves

FREEZING HINT

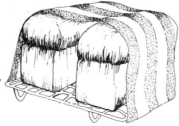

Home-baked crusty bread is less likely to 'shell off' its crust when frozen if you allow the cooked bread to cool while covered lightly with a clean tea towel.

You will need . . .

1 (850-g/1 lb 14-oz) pack brown bread mix
75 g/3 oz butter
1 teaspoon dried mixed herbs (optional)
1 tablespoon chopped parsley or tarragon (optional)
625 ml/generous 1 pint hot water
little milk for brushing

Cooking time
about 15 minutes

Oven setting
220°C, 425°F, Gas Mark 7

Storage time
6 weeks

Defrosting time
3 hours at room temperature

Place the bread mix in a large bowl and rub in the butter. Stir in the herbs, if liked. Add the hot water. This should be as hot as the hand can stand. Beat with a wooden spoon or by hand until the water is absorbed. Turn out on a floured surface and knead for at least 5 minutes.

Divide into 50-g/2-oz pieces and shape each into a rope about 15 cm/6 inches long. Tie each rope into a single knot. Arrange the knots, all pointing in one direction, on greased baking sheets, allowing a small space between each. When risen and baked the rolls should be just touching. Brush with milk.

Cover the shaped rolls with greased polythene and allow to rise until double in size. Bake in a hot oven for about 15 minutes. Cool.

To freeze: Pack in batches in polythene bags. Seal and label.
To serve: Defrost in the sealed pack. Toast lightly if required warm.
Makes 24

FREEZING HINT

To heat up frozen rolls and make the crusty part crisp, sprinkle them with cold water before putting in the oven in the frozen state.

161 Basic muffins

You will need . . .

Cooking time
20–25 minutes

Oven setting
230°C, 450°F, Gas Mark 8

Storage time
4–6 months

Defrosting time
10 minutes in the oven from frozen

675 g/1½ lb plain flour
3 tablespoons baking powder
½ teaspoon salt
75 g/3 oz castor sugar
3 eggs, beaten
750 ml/1¼ pints milk
100 g/4 oz butter, melted
lard for greasing tins

Sift the flour, baking powder and salt into a bowl. Stir in the sugar. Beat together the eggs, milk and melted butter and pour into the dry ingredients. Stir the mixture only until just moistened. Divide into three equal portions.

Use one portion of the mixture and divide between 12 deep bun tins, greased with lard, filling them two-thirds full. Bake in a hot oven for 20–25 minutes, until risen and golden brown. Cool on a wire tray.

To freeze: Pack 6 muffins together in two foil parcels. Seal and label.
To serve: Place the parcels, still sealed and frozen, on a baking sheet and defrost in a hot oven for 10 minutes. Serve warm.
Makes 12

FREEZING HINT

Muffins served with a hot main dish, American fashion, are delicious. Make a few, omitting the sugar, and freeze ready to use for this purpose.

Hot banana
162 and nut muffins

You will need . . .

Cooking time
20–25 minutes

Oven setting
200°C, 400°F, Gas Mark 6
230°C, 450°F, Gas Mark 8

Storage time
4–6 months

Defrosting time
12 minutes in the oven from frozen

50 g/2 oz butter
75 g/3 oz castor sugar
1 egg
200 g/7 oz plain flour
2 teaspoons baking powder
¼ teaspoon bicarbonate of soda
¾ teaspoon salt
3 ripe bananas, mashed
50 g/2 oz walnuts, chopped
lard for greasing tins

Cream together the butter and sugar until light and fluffy. Gradually beat in the egg. Sift together the flour, baking powder, bicarbonate of soda and salt and fold into the creamed mixture alternately with the mashed bananas.

Mix lightly until the batter is smooth. Stir in the nuts.

Divide the mixture between 12 deep bun tins greased with lard, filling them two-thirds full. Bake in a moderately hot oven for 20–25 minutes, until well risen and golden brown. Cool on a wire tray.

To freeze: Pack 6 muffins together in foil parcels. Seal and label.
To serve: Place the parcels, still sealed and frozen, on a baking sheet and defrost in a hot oven for 12 minutes. Serve hot.
Makes 12

FREEZING HINT

When you freeze French bread, cut the ends off the loaves as this helps to prevent the crust from shelling off.

Apple spice muffins and
163 Herby cheese muffins

Sultana
164 wheatgerm muffins

You will need . . .

2 portions basic muffin mix (see recipe 161)
lard for greasing tins
For the Apple spice muffins:
175 g/6 oz grated cooking apples
pinch ground cinnamon
pinch ground nutmeg
½ teaspoon grated lemon zest
For the Herby cheese muffins:
1 tablespoon chopped parsley
50 g/2 oz cheese, grated
pinch dry mustard

Cooking time
20—25 minutes

Oven setting
230°C, 450°F, Gas Mark 8

Storage time
4—6 months

Defrosting time
10 minutes in the oven from frozen

To make the Apple spice muffins, mix together the grated apple, spices and lemon zest. Stir gently into one portion of the basic muffin mix.

To make the Herby cheese muffins, mix together the chopped parsley, grated cheese and mustard. Stir lightly into the remaining portion of muffin mix.

Divide the mixtures between 24 greased deep bun tins, filling them two-thirds full, to make 12 Apple spice muffins and 12 Herby cheese muffins. Bake in a hot oven for 20—25 minutes. Cool on a wire tray.

To freeze: Pack 6 muffins together in foil parcels. Seal and label.
To serve: Place the parcels, still sealed and frozen, on a baking sheet and defrost in a hot oven for 10 minutes. Serve warm.
Makes 24

You will need . . .

1 egg, beaten
25 g/1 oz butter, melted
175 ml/6 fl oz milk
75 g/3 oz clear honey
150 g/5 oz plain flour
1 tablespoon baking powder
½ teaspoon salt
50 g/2 oz wheatgerm
75 g/3 oz sultanas
lard for greasing tins

Cooking time
20—25 minutes

Oven setting
220°C, 425°F, Gas Mark 7

Storage time
4—6 months

Defrosting time
10 minutes in the oven from frozen

Mix together the egg, melted butter, milk and honey. Sift the flour, baking powder and salt into a bowl and stir in the wheatgerm. Pour in the honey mixture.

Stir only until the dry ingredients are moistened. Fold in the sultanas.

Divide between 12 greased deep bun tins, filling them two-thirds full. Bake in a hot oven for 20—25 minutes, until well risen and browned. Cool on a wire tray.

To freeze: Pack 6 muffins together in foil parcels. Seal and label.
To serve: Place the parcels, still sealed and frozen, on a baking sheet and defrost in a hot oven for 10 minutes. Serve warm.
Makes 12

FREEZING HINT

Fruits which discolour soon after the skin is removed should be prepared quickly for freezing; remember also that discoloration takes place more rapidly than usual when the fruit is defrosted, so it is better to serve it cooked, or, if raw, while still chilled.

FREEZING HINT

Buy 2 or more varieties of sliced bread packs of the same size. Open the packs carefully, mix them or divide into smaller quantities, reassemble and seal. You can bring them out one mixed pack at a time.

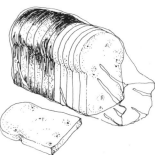

Basic
165 potato bread rolls

Marmalade buns
166 and Apricot nut rolls

You will need . . .

1 (85-g/3-oz) packet instant potato
250 ml/8 fl oz milk
100 g/4 oz margarine
50 g/2 oz sugar
1 teaspoon salt
2 teaspoons dried yeast
2 eggs, beaten
725 g/1 lb 10 oz strong plain flour

Cooking time
10–12 minutes

Oven setting
220°C, 425°F, Gas Mark 7

Storage time
2 months

Defrosting time
3 hours at room temperature

Make up the potato with 350 ml/12 fl oz boiling water. Mix with the milk, margarine, sugar and salt. Stir to melt the margarine then cool to lukewarm. Dissolve the yeast in 100 ml/4 fl oz lukewarm water and add to the mixture with the eggs. Add 175 g/6 oz flour and beat until smooth. Cover and stand in a warm place for about 2 hours, until full of bubbles.

Add sufficient flour to make a stiff dough. Turn out and knead for 5 minutes. Cover with greased polythene, allow to rise until double in bulk then knead again for 1 minute. Divide into two equal portions. Shape one portion into a roll and cut into 18 pieces. Roll each piece to a long sausage shape and twist lightly. Lay on greased baking trays, cover with greased polythene and allow to rise until double in size. Brush with a little salt dissolved in hot water. Bake in a hot oven for 10–12 minutes. Cool.

To freeze: Pack in foil. Seal and label.
To serve: Defrost while still sealed in the pack.
Makes 18

FREEZING HINT

To make sure that cheese which has been stored in the freezer regains full flavour, defrost it still sealed in the pack and allow to come fully up to room temperature before serving.

You will need . . .

1 portion potato bread roll dough
For the marmalade filling:
100 g/4 oz thick cut marmalade
1 cooking apple, grated
For the apricot nut filling:
100 g/4 oz drained canned apricots
50 g/2 oz chopped toasted hazelnuts
25 g/1 oz soft brown sugar
25 g/1 oz butter, melted
pinch ground nutmeg

Cooking time
20–25 minutes

Oven setting
200°C, 400°F, Gas Mark 6

Storage time
2 months

Defrosting time
3 hours at room temperature
and 10 minutes in the oven

Mix together the marmalade and apple. Roll out half the dough to a rectangle about 30 × 23 cm/12 × 9 inches. Spread with the marmalade mixture and roll up. Cut into 9 equal slices. Lay in buttered deep bun tins. Cover with greased polythene and allow to rise until double in size.

Chop the apricots and mix with the hazelnuts, brown sugar, butter and nutmeg. Divide the remaining dough into 9 equal pieces and shape each into a round ball. Flatten and place on a spoonful of apricot filling. Gather in the edges, dampen and seal well together. Place the rolls, joins underneath, in buttered deep bun tins. Cover with greased polythene and allow to rise until doubled. Bake in a moderately hot oven for 20–25 minutes. Cool.

To freeze: Pack in polythene bags. Seal and label.
To serve: Unpack and arrange on a baking tray to defrost. Warm through in a moderately hot oven for 10 minutes.
Makes 18

FREEZING HINT

Seville oranges have a short season but they freeze perfectly. This allows you to make marmalade later in the year when it is convenient. Wash and dry them and pack in polythene bags.

Grated
167 potato pancakes

168 Potato scones

You will need . . .

1 kg/2 lb potatoes
1 small onion
2 eggs, beaten
3 tablespoons flour
pinch ground nutmeg
pinch pepper
1 teaspoon salt
½ teaspoon baking powder
little butter for cooking
When serving:
parsley

Cooking time
10–15 minutes

Storage time
4–6 months

Defrosting time
4 hours at room temperature
and about 4 minutes in the
frying pan

Peel and finely grate the raw potatoes and onion into a
bowl and leave to stand for about 10 minutes. Drain off
any liquid which collects in the bowl.

Add the eggs and all other ingredients to the bowl and
beat well until smooth.

Melt a little butter in a heavy frying pan and heat
through evenly. Drop the batter, in spoonfuls, into the
hot pan and fry for about 2–3 minutes. Turn the pancakes
and fry for a further 2–3 minutes, until golden brown.
Drain well on kitchen paper and cool.

To freeze: Pack in polythene or foil containers in layers
with dividers. Seal and label.
To serve: Defrost in the pack then heat through on both
sides in a frying pan just smeared with butter. Garnish with
parsley.
Makes about 20

You will need . . .

450 g/1 lb potatoes, peeled
50 g/2 oz butter
1 teaspoon salt
1 egg yolk
about 100 g/4 oz flour
little butter for cooking

Cooking time
about 30 minutes

Storage time
4–6 months

Defrosting time
about 6 minutes under the
grill

Boil the potatoes in salted water until cooked. Drain and
mash well until completely smooth. Beat in the butter,
salt and egg yolk and sufficient flour to give a stiff dough.

Turn the mixture on to a floured surface and knead
lightly until smooth. Roll out to a 5 mm/¼ inch thickness
and cut into 15-cm/6-inch circles. Cut each circle into four,
to make scones.

Lightly grease a heavy frying pan or girdle and heat
through evenly. Cook the scones for 3–4 minutes on each
side. Cool.

To freeze: Pack in polythene bags. Seal and label.
To serve: Unpack and place still frozen under a hot
grill. Toast for about 3 minutes on each side, until heated
through and browned. Serve with butter and preserves.
Makes 8–10

FREEZING HINT

*Used polythene bags can still be
of use, even if punctured. Wash
and cut up to make dividers.*

FREEZING HINT

*These scones are delicious if fried
from frozen in bacon fat or butter
to serve with bacon for breakfast.*

You will need . . .

450 g/1 lb plain flour
1 teaspoon salt
1 teaspoon bicarbonate of soda
2 teaspoons cream of tartar
100 g/4 oz margarine
about 300 ml/½ pint milk
1 egg, beaten
For the Blackberry secrets:
about 100 g/4 oz frozen blackberries, defrosted
50 g/2 oz castor sugar
little milk for brushing

Cooking time
7–10 minutes

Oven setting
220°C, 425°F, Gas Mark 7
200°C, 400°F, Gas Mark 6

Storage time
4–6 months

Defrosting time
10 minutes in the oven from frozen

You will need . . .

100 g/4 oz wholemeal flour
100 g/4 oz plain flour
pinch salt
1 teaspoon bicarbonate of soda
1 teaspoon cream of tartar
50 g/2 oz lard
2 teaspoons castor sugar
about 150 ml/¼ pint buttermilk

Cooking time
about 10 minutes

Oven setting
220°C, 425°F, Gas Mark 7
200°C, 400°F, Gas Mark 6

Storage time
4–6 months

Defrosting time
10 minutes in the oven from frozen

Sift the flour with the salt, bicarbonate of soda and cream of tartar. Rub in the margarine. Add sufficient milk to form a soft dough and divide into two portions.

Pat out one portion to a thickness of 2.5 cm/1 inch and cut into 9 rounds with a 5-cm/2-inch biscuit cutter. Place on a greased baking tray and brush with beaten egg. Bake in a hot oven for 7–10 minutes.

Pat out the remaining dough to a thickness of 1 cm/½ inch and cut into 18 rounds as above. Top half the rounds with three sugared berries each then cover with the remaining rounds. Moisten the edges and pinch together to seal. Brush with milk and bake as above.

To freeze: Pack in polythene bags. Seal and label.
To serve: Unpack and place frozen scones on a baking sheet. Reheat in a moderately hot oven for 10 minutes. Dust the Blackberry secrets with icing sugar, if liked.
Makes 18

Sift the flours with the salt, bicarbonate of soda and cream of tartar into a bowl and rub in the lard. Stir in the sugar and enough buttermilk to make a soft dough. Turn out on a floured surface and knead lightly.

Pat out to a thickness of about 2 cm/¾ inch and cut into 12 triangles. Place on a greased baking sheet and dust lightly with flour. Bake in a hot oven for about 10 minutes. Cool.

To freeze: Pack in a polythene bag. Seal and label.
To serve: Unpack and place on a baking sheet. Reheat from frozen in a moderately hot oven for about 10 minutes.
Makes 12

FREEZING HINT

Plain or fruit scones can be frozen to use for tea with butter and jam. Underbake slightly, cool and pack in a polythene bag. While still frozen, place scones on a baking sheet and allow time to defrost and reheat in the oven.

FREEZING HINT

Save plastic clips from polythene bread bags to seal your own packs for freezing.

Cheese
171 and corn square

172 Sweet pinwheel scones

You will need . . .

Cooking time
12–15 minutes

Oven setting
220°C, 425°F, Gas Mark 7
200°C, 400°F, Gas Mark 6

Storage time
4–6 months

Defrosting time
15 minutes in the oven from frozen

350 g/12 oz plain flour
½ teaspoon salt
pinch dry mustard
4 teaspoons baking powder
½ teaspoon cream of tartar
200 g/7 oz butter
100 g/4 oz canned sweetcorn kernels
200 ml/7 fl oz milk or tomato juice
175 g/6 oz Cheddar cheese, grated

Sift the flour, salt, mustard, baking powder and cream of tartar into a bowl and rub in 150 g/5 oz of the butter. Stir in the well-drained sweetcorn kernels and add sufficient milk or tomato juice to form a soft dough.

Place on a floured surface and knead ten times. Roll out to a thickness of 1 cm/½ inch and cut into 25 rounds with a 5-cm/2-inch biscuit cutter. Place the rounds together in a greased 23-cm/9-inch square foil container. Melt the cheese and remaining butter carefully in a saucepan over gentle heat. Trickle this mixture over the tops of the scones and bake in a hot oven for 12–15 minutes. Cool.

To freeze: Cover with lid or foil. Seal and label.
To serve: Uncover and reheat in a moderately hot oven. Pull apart and serve with butter.
Makes 25

You will need . . .

Cooking time
15–20 minutes

Oven setting
220°C, 425°F, Gas Mark 7

Storage time
4–6 months

Defrosting time
1 hour at room temperature

225 g/8 oz self-raising flour
2 teaspoons baking powder
150 g/5 oz butter
1 egg, beaten
50 ml/2 fl oz milk
75 g/3 oz soft brown sugar
1 teaspoon ground cinnamon

Sift the flour and baking powder into a bowl and rub in 100 g/4 oz of the butter. Add the egg and sufficient milk to make a soft dough. Turn out on a floured surface and knead lightly. Roll out to a rectangle about 30 × 15 cm/ 12 × 6 inches. Melt the remaining butter and use to brush the dough. Mix together the brown sugar and cinnamon and sprinkle over the top. Roll up from the long side and cut into 12 slices. Place the slices on a greased baking sheet and bake in a hot oven for 15–20 minutes. Cool.

To freeze: Pack in a rigid container with dividers. Seal and label.
To serve: Unpack and arrange on a serving dish to defrost.
Makes 12

FREEZING HINT

Keep an emergency pint of homogenised milk in the freezer, but if it is not in a carton repack it in a polythene container, leaving headspace for expansion.

FREEZING HINT

Savoury scones are as easy to make as sweet ones. Just substitute cream cheese, well-seasoned with celery salt or caraway seeds, for the sugar and cinnamon filling.

173 Irish soda bread

Overnight
174 oatmeal bread

You will need . . .

Cooking time
25–30 minutes

Oven setting
200°C, 400°F, Gas Mark 6

Storage time
4–6 months

Defrosting time
4 hours at room temperature
or 45 minutes in the oven
from frozen

675 g/1½ lb plain flour
1½ teaspoons salt
1½ teaspoons bicarbonate of soda
50 g/2 oz butter
450 ml/¾ pint milk
1½ teaspoons cream of tartar

Sift the flour with the salt and bicarbonate of soda into a
bowl. Rub in the butter.

Mix together the milk and cream of tartar and pour
into the dry ingredients. Mix well to form a soft dough.

Shape the dough into a round and place on a floured
baking tray. Score the round into quarters and bake in
a moderately hot oven for 25–30 minutes, until the loaf
sounds hollow when tapped on the base. Cool.

To freeze: Pack in a polythene bag. Seal and label.
To serve: Defrost at room temperature while still wrapped.
If required quickly place frozen loaf, wrapped in foil,
in a moderately hot oven for 35 minutes, then uncover
and bake for a further 10 minutes to crisp the crust.

You will need . . .

Cooking time
45 minutes

Oven setting
220°C, 425°F, Gas Mark 7
190°C, 375°F, Gas Mark 5

Storage time
2 months

Defrosting time
4 hours at room temperature

275 g/10 oz fine or medium oatmeal
3 tablespoons black treacle
2 tablespoons clear honey
1 tablespoon salt
40 g/1½ oz margarine
600 ml/1 pint boiling water
15 g/½ oz dried yeast
2 teaspoons sugar
150 ml/¼ pint warm water
675 g/1½ lb wholemeal flour

In a large bowl mix the oatmeal, treacle, honey, salt, margarine and boiling water. Cool to lukewarm. Dissolve the
yeast and sugar in the warm water. Allow to stand for 10
minutes until frothy, then stir into the oatmeal mixture. Beat
in the flour to make a sticky dough, then turn out and knead
for 8–10 minutes. Place in a greased bowl and cover with
greased polythene. Refrigerate overnight.

Next day, knead lightly for 1 minute then allow to rise
in a warm place until double in bulk. Knock back the
dough, divide in half and shape to fit a greased 1-kg/2-lb
loaf tin and 18-cm/7-inch round cake tin. Prove in a
warm place until double in bulk. Sprinkle with wholemeal
flour, if liked. Bake in a hot oven for 15 minutes, then
reduce to moderately hot for a further 30 minutes. Cool
on a wire tray.

To freeze: Pack in foil or polythene bags. Seal and label.
To serve: Defrost at room temperature while still wrapped.
Makes 2 loaves

FREEZING HINT

*Leftover stale bread reduced to
breadcrumbs in a blender can be
stored in small containers, and
does not even need to be
thawed before use.*

FREEZING HINT

*When trimming sandwiches to
make packs for the freezer, save
the crusts. Cut into small pieces
and fry in butter until crisp and
golden. Cool, then freeze and use
as a garnish for vegetable soups;
the different flavours from the
sandwich fillings add interest.*

175 Raisin batter bread

You will need . . .

Cooking time
about 30 minutes

Oven setting
200°C, 400°F, Gas Mark 6

Storage time
2 months

Defrosting time
4 hours at room temperature

50 g/2 oz butter
100 g/4 oz sugar
1 teaspoon salt
150 ml/¼ pint hot water
100 ml/4 fl oz warm water
4 teaspoons dried yeast
1 egg
425 g/15 oz plain flour
175 g/6 oz seedless raisins

Mix together the butter, sugar, salt and hot water until the butter melts. Leave until lukewarm. Pour the warm water into a warmed mixing bowl and sprinkle on the yeast. Stir until dissolved then add the butter mixture. Beat the egg, add to the bowl with the flour and raisins and stir with a wooden spoon for about 2 minutes, until smooth.

Cover and allow to rise until double in bulk. Beat for 30 seconds then divide between two greased 1-kg/2-lb loaf tins. Bake in a moderately hot oven for about 30 minutes. Cool.

To freeze: Pack in polythene bags. Seal and label.
To serve: Defrost in the sealed pack. Serve sliced with butter.
Makes 2 loaves

FREEZING HINT

To keep a sandwich meal cool until lunchtime, pack a drink in a sealed tumbler, still in the frozen state, inside the lunch pack. As the drink thaws, it keeps the food cool.

176 Sweet bubble bread

You will need . . .

Cooking time
about 30 minutes

Oven setting
190°C, 375°F, Gas Mark 5

Storage time
2 months

Defrosting time
4 hours at room temperature

75 g/3 oz soft margarine
350–450 g/12 oz–1 lb plain flour
½ teaspoon salt
2 teaspoons dried yeast
50 g/2 oz castor sugar
1 egg
100 g/4 oz butter, melted
100 g/4 oz soft brown sugar
½ teaspoon ground cinnamon

Soften the margarine in a large bowl. Add 75 g/3 oz flour, the salt, yeast and castor sugar. Pour 175 ml/6 fl oz of very hot water into the bowl and beat well for 2 minutes. Add a further 75 g/3 oz flour and the egg and beat again for 2 minutes. Add sufficient of the remaining flour to make a soft dough.

Turn out and knead for 8 minutes. Grease the bowl, return the dough and cover with greased polythene. Allow to rise until doubled in bulk then divide in half.

Shape each portion into a roll, cut into 24 equal pieces and form the pieces into balls. Dip in the melted butter, roll in the mixed brown sugar and cinnamon and place 24 in each of two greased 1-kg/2-lb loaf tins. Sprinkle over any remaining sugar mixture. Cover with greased polythene and allow to rise until double in size. Bake in a moderately hot oven for about 30 minutes. Cool.

To freeze: Pack in polythene bags. Seal and label.
To serve: Defrost while still sealed in the pack.
Makes 2 loaves

FREEZING HINT

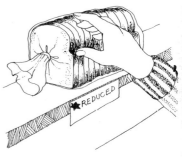

Bread is often sold off cheaply just before shops close for the weekend, as it would be stale by Monday. Bag it or wrap quickly in foil and pop into the freezer; the fresher it is frozen the better it will taste when defrosted.

177 Plain drop scones

You will need . . .

Cooking time
about 10 minutes

Storage time
4–6 months

Defrosting time
1–2 hours at room
temperature

100 g/4 oz plain flour
½ teaspoon bicarbonate of soda
1 teaspoon cream of tartar
25 g/1 oz sugar
1 egg
150 ml/¼ pint milk
2 tablespoons corn oil
little oil for cooking

Sift the flour with the bicarbonate of soda and cream of
tartar. Stir in the sugar. Beat together the egg, milk and
oil and pour into the dry ingredients. Whisk or beat until
the batter is smooth.

Very lightly oil a heavy frying pan or girdle and heat
through evenly. Carefully pour in the batter, a tablespoon
at a time, to make neat round scones. When the tops are
covered with bubbles, turn the scones and brown the
other sides.

Place the hot cooked scones on a plate and cover with
a clean teacloth. Cool.

To freeze: Pack in foil or polythene bags. Seal and label.
To serve: Unpack, spread out on a serving plate and
cover with another plate or a polythene bag to defrost.
Serve cold with butter and preserves.
Makes 10–12

FREEZING HINT

*To make fruit drop scones, pour
the batter into the hot pan and
sprinkle on a few currants before
turning to brown the other side.*

178 Savoury girdle scones

You will need . . .

Cooking time
about 10 minutes

Oven setting
190°C, 375°F, Gas Mark 5

Storage time
4–6 months

Defrosting time
20 minutes in the oven from
frozen

100 g/4 oz plain flour
pinch salt
pinch cayenne pepper
pinch ground allspice
2 tablespoons grated Parmesan cheese
1 egg
25 g/1 oz butter, melted
150 ml/¼ pint milk
little butter for cooking
When serving:
parsley

Sift the flour with the salt, pepper and allspice into a bowl
and stir in the Parmesan cheese. Beat together the egg,
butter and milk and pour into the dry ingredients. Whisk
or beat until the batter is smooth.

Lightly butter a heavy frying pan or girdle and heat
through evenly. Drop in spoonfuls of the batter, being
careful not to crowd the pan, and when the top of each
scone is covered with bubbles, turn over and brown the
other side.

Place the scones together on a plate and cover with a
clean teacloth. Cool.

To freeze: Pack in two foil parcels. Seal and label.
To serve: Place the sealed packs on a baking tray and
reheat from frozen in a moderately hot oven for about
20 minutes. Serve warm with soft liver pâté or seasoned
cream cheese, if liked, and garnish with parsley.
Makes 10–12

FREEZING HINT

*If you have some soft butter
available, it takes little time to
flavour it with chopped parsley or
other herbs and a little lemon
juice. Seal it in foil in the shape of
a roll, and when required cut slices
from the frozen roll as butter pats.*

179 Treacle scones

You will need . . .

Cooking time
7–8 minutes

Oven setting
180°C, 350°F, Gas Mark 4

Storage time
4–6 months

Defrosting time
30 minutes at room
temperature or 15 minutes
in the oven from frozen

175 g/6 oz plain flour
pinch salt
4 teaspoons baking powder
50 g/2 oz rolled oats
50 g/2 oz soft margarine
2 tablespoons black treacle
4 tablespoons milk
little butter for cooking

Sift the flour, salt and baking powder into a bowl. Stir
in the oats and rub in the margarine. Beat in the treacle
and milk to make a soft dough.

Roll out the dough on a floured surface and cut into
triangles.

Lightly grease a heavy frying pan or girdle and heat
through evenly. Cook the scones for about 4 minutes then
turn over and cook the other sides for 3–4 minutes. Cool.

To freeze: Pack in a polythene bag. Seal and label.
To serve: Unpack and spread out on a serving dish to
defrost. If required quickly, place still frozen on a baking
tray and reheat in a moderate oven for 15 minutes.
Makes 8

FREEZING HINT

*To add a quick cobbler topping to
a casserole, have ready in the
freezer small bags of partly cooked
scones. Arrange these, still frozen,
on top, and they will defrost and
cook through in the same time it
would take to cook fresh scones.*

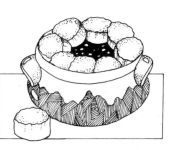

180 Cornmeal girdle cakes

You will need . . .

Cooking time
about 30 minutes

Oven setting
200°C, 400°F, Gas Mark 6

Storage time
4–6 months

Defrosting time
1–2 hours at room
temperature and 7 minutes
in the oven

150 g/5 oz plain flour
½ teaspoon salt
1 tablespoon baking powder
75 g/3 oz cornmeal (maize meal)
2 eggs, beaten
1 tablespoon black treacle
2 tablespoons corn oil
about 350 ml/12 fl oz milk
little butter for cooking

Sift the flour, salt and baking powder into a bowl and
stir in the cornmeal. Mix together the eggs, treacle, oil
and half the milk and pour into the dry ingredients. Beat
until blended then gradually add more milk, until the
mixture is the consistency of double cream.

Lightly butter a heavy frying pan or girdle and heat
through. Pour a tablespoon of the batter from the tip of a
spoon to make a round pancake. When the top is covered
with small bubbles, turn and brown the other side. Add a
little milk or flour if the batter is not the right consistency.
Stack the cooked pancakes on a plate and cover. Cool.

To freeze: Pack in polythene bags. Seal and label.
To serve: Defrost in the sealed pack. Place on a greased
baking tray and brush with melted butter. Reheat in a
moderately hot oven for about 7 minutes. Serve with butter
and maple syrup.
Makes 16–20

FREEZING HINT

*Rolls need only be partially baked
before freezing; just sufficiently to
prevent over-proving and 'set' the
bread. There is then no danger of
over-browning them when
defrosting, and reheating. When
required, place frozen rolls in a
hot oven for 15 minutes.*

181 Spiced parsnip loaf

You will need . . .

Cooking time
about 1 hour

Oven setting
180°C, 350°F, Gas Mark 4

Storage time
4–6 months

Defrosting time
4 hours at room temperature

100 g/4 oz soft margarine
150 g/5 oz soft brown sugar
2 eggs, beaten
1 teaspoon vanilla essence
225 g/8 oz plain flour
1 teaspoon bicarbonate of soda
1 teaspoon salt
1 teaspoon ground cinnamon
$\frac{1}{2}$ teaspoon ground nutmeg
$\frac{1}{4}$ teaspoon ground cloves
1 tablespoon vinegar
225 g/8 oz parsnip, finely grated

Cream the margarine and sugar together until light and fluffy. Gradually beat in the eggs and vanilla essence. Sift the flour with the bicarbonate of soda, salt and spices.

Make the vinegar up to 100 ml/4 fl oz with water and add to the creamed mixture alternately with the grated parsnip and the flour.

Turn the mixture into a greased 1-kg/2-lb loaf tin and bake in a moderate oven for about 1 hour. Cool on a wire tray.

To freeze: Pack in a polythene bag. Seal and label.
To serve: Defrost while still wrapped. Serve thinly sliced with butter.

FREEZING HINT

Foods frozen in a number of boiling bags can be reheated together in a large pan of boiling water to make a complete meal.

182 Frying pan teacake

You will need . . .

Cooking time
10 minutes

Storage time
4–6 months

Defrosting time
3 hours at room temperature and 6 minutes under the grill

350 g/12 oz plain flour
$\frac{1}{2}$ teaspoon ground cinnamon
pinch salt
1 teaspoon cream of tartar
$\frac{1}{2}$ teaspoon bicarbonate of soda
75 g/3 oz lard
150 g/5 oz currants or sultanas
225 ml/7$\frac{1}{2}$ fl oz fresh or sour milk

Sift the flour with the cinnamon, salt, cream of tartar and bicarbonate of soda into a bowl. Rub in the lard and stir in the dried fruit. Mix to a fairly soft dough with the milk.

Turn out on a floured surface and form into a round flat cake about 5 mm/$\frac{1}{4}$ inch thick.

Heat a heavy frying pan and sprinkle with flour. Put in the cake and cook over medium heat for 5 minutes, until golden brown. Turn the cake over and cook for a further 5 minutes. Cool.

To freeze: Pack in foil or a polythene bag. Seal and label.
To serve: Defrost in the pack. Unwrap and toast the cake lightly on both sides. Serve split through and buttered.

FREEZING HINT

Freeze mixed bunches of herbs, with the stalks tied together, in packs to use as bouquets garnis.

183 Standing tcabread

You will need . . .

Cooking time
1¼–1½ hours

Oven setting
180°C, 350°F, Gas Mark 4

Storage time
4–6 months

Defrosting time
4 hours at room temperature

100 g/4 oz plain flour
2½ teaspoons baking powder
½ teaspoon bicarbonate of soda
1 teaspoon salt
225 g/8 oz wholemeal flour
2 tablespoons soft brown sugar
175 ml/6 fl oz milk
175 ml/6 fl oz water
250 g/9 oz black treacle
100 g/4 oz hazelnuts, chopped

Sift the plain flour with the baking powder, bicarbonate of soda and salt and stir in the wholemeal flour and sugar.

Mix together the milk, water and treacle and stir well. Pour the treacle mixture into the dry ingredients and beat until smooth. Stir in the nuts.

Pour the mixture into a greased 1-kg/2-lb loaf tin and allow to stand for 20 minutes. Bake in a moderate oven for 1¼–1½ hours. Cool in the tin for 10 minutes then turn out on a wire tray.

To freeze: Pack in a polythene bag or wrap in foil. Seal and label.
To serve: Defrost while still wrapped. Serve thinly sliced with butter.

184 Chopped peanut loaf

You will need . . .

Cooking time
1 hour

Oven setting
180°C, 350°F, Gas Mark 4

Storage time
4–6 months

Defrosting time
4 hours at room temperature

100 g/4 oz wholemeal flour
100 g/4 oz plain flour
2 teaspoons baking powder
¼ teaspoon salt
100 g/4 oz peanut butter
1 egg
3 tablespoons clear honey
250 ml/8 fl oz milk
25 g/1 oz margarine, melted
1 teaspoon grated lemon zest
50 g/2 oz salted peanuts, chopped

Mix together the flours, baking powder and salt in a large bowl. Rub in the peanut butter until the mixture is crumbly.

Lightly beat the egg and add to the flour mixture with the honey, milk, melted margarine and lemon zest. Stir until just combined then fold in the chopped peanuts.

Spoon the mixture into a 1-kg/2-lb loaf tin and bake in a moderate oven for 1 hour. Cool for 10 minutes in the tin, then turn out on to a wire rack.

To freeze: Wrap in foil or a polythene bag. Seal and label.
To serve: Defrost, still wrapped, at room temperature. Serve sliced with butter and honey.

FREEZING HINT

Freezer foil is worth salvaging for re-use. To prevent it from tearing when you clean it, soak in very hot water with washing-up liquid. Lift out, shake dry and lay on a flat surface covered with a clean tea towel. Smooth it with another tea towel folded into a pad.

FREEZING HINT

When moving house, ensure that the freezer is the last item into the removal van and the first off at the end of the journey. Also that it is fitted with a plug to connect to a suitable socket in the new house.

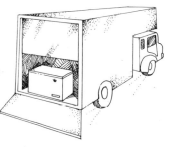

Cakes and cookies

Keeping the family supplied with everyday cakes can be quite a task. Even sweet biscuits are expensive to buy and never seem quite so delectable as those you bake yourself. And yet a small amount of dough can produce as many as 40 cookies. Tray cakes are very little trouble to make, using a roasting tin, and can be cut up afterwards into large or small shapes, according to your needs.

To widen the range, I have included no-bake cakes, where the melting method is used. Then there are unusual recipes for ring cakes, which turn out easily from a ring tin, and look most effective when decorated.

185 Strawberry squares

(illustrated on back of jacket)

You will need . . .

Cooking time
15 minutes

Oven setting
180°C, 350°F, Gas Mark 4

Storage time
4–6 months

Defrosting time
15 minutes at room temperature

100 g/4 oz plain flour
40 g/1½ oz soft brown sugar
50 g/2 oz walnuts, chopped
100 g/4 oz butter, melted
2 egg whites
225 g/8 oz castor sugar
150 g/5 oz fresh or frozen strawberries, chopped
2 tablespoons lemon juice
300 ml/½ pint double cream

Mix together the flour, brown sugar and walnuts. Stir in the melted butter then spread the mixture in two Swiss roll tins. Bake in a moderate oven for 15 minutes. Cool. Whisk the egg whites until stiff. Gradually whisk in the castor sugar, strawberries and lemon juice, until thick and creamy. Whip the cream and fold in. Crumble the cooled walnut mixture and sprinkle half over the bases of two 18-cm/ 7-inch shaped foil containers. Divide the strawberry cream mixture between the containers. Sprinkle the remaining crumbs on top and press down lightly.

To freeze: Cover with lid. Seal and label.
To serve: Uncover container and defrost. Cut into squares.
Makes 32

186 Walnut brownies

You will need . . .

Cooking time
50–55 minutes

Oven setting
160°C, 325°F, Gas Mark 3

Storage time
4–6 months

Defrosting time
1 hour at room temperature

100 g/4 oz self-raising flour
1 teaspoon baking powder
75 g/3 oz cocoa powder
50 g/2 oz ground almonds
450 g/1 lb soft brown sugar
225 g/8 oz soft margarine
75 g/3 oz chopped walnuts
3 eggs
4 tablespoons milk
When serving:
icing sugar to sprinkle

Sift the flour with the baking powder and cocoa into a bowl. Add all the other ingredients and beat until well blended.

Spread the mixture in an 18-cm/7-inch square tin lined with foil or non-stick paper and bake in a moderate oven for 50–55 minutes.

Allow to cool completely in the tin then cut into 5-cm/ 2-inch squares.

To freeze: Pack in rigid containers with dividers. Seal and label.
To serve: Unpack and spread out on a serving plate to defrost. Dust lightly with icing sugar.
Makes 16

FREEZING HINT

Syrup left over from serving fruit frozen in sugar syrup can be whisked into custard as it cools to produce a quick and delicious fruit-flavoured sauce.

FREEZING HINT

Sugar, particularly brown sugar, tends to form a solid block when stored in a kitchen cupboard. Avoid this by keeping your sugar in a sealed carton in the freezer.

Coffee
187 and orange diamonds

You will need . . .

Cooking time
55–60 minutes

Oven setting
180°C, 350°F, Gas Mark 4

Storage time
4–6 months

Defrosting time
Whole cake – 4 hours at room temperature
Portions – 1 hour

225 g/8 oz butter
225 g/8 oz castor sugar
4 eggs
2 tablespoons coffee essence
225 g/8 oz self-raising flour
For the buttercream:
50 g/2 oz butter
350 g/12 oz icing sugar, sifted
1 egg yolk
juice and zest of 1 orange
When serving:
orange jelly slices

Cream the butter and sugar until light. Beat in the eggs, one at a time, then the coffee essence. Fold in the flour with a metal spoon and turn into a lined and greased 30 × 25-cm/12 × 10-inch roasting tin. Bake in a moderate oven for 55–60 minutes. Cool on a wire tray.

Make the buttercream. Beat the butter with half the sugar until smooth. Add the egg yolk, then gradually beat in the rest of the sugar, the grated orange zest and 2 tablespoons juice. Swirl over the top of the cake and mark into diamonds.

To freeze: Open freeze the cake whole, or cut into diamonds before freezing. When solid, pack in a single layer in foil or polythene containers. Seal and label.
To serve: Uncover to defrost. Cut into diamonds if necessary and decorate with orange jelly slices.
Makes 20–24

FREEZING HINT

The easiest buttercream to spread while semi-frozen is made by creaming 175 g/6 oz soft margarine with 75 g/3 oz sifted icing sugar and beating in 2 egg yolks. Extra sugar makes the consistency firmer if required.

188 Italian marbled cake

You will need . . .

Cooking time
40–45 minutes

Oven setting
180°C, 350°F, Gas Mark 4

Storage time
4–6 months

Defrosting time
1 hour at room temperature

75 g/3 oz butter
175 g/6 oz plain flour
pinch salt
6 eggs
225 g/8 oz castor sugar
1 teaspoon almond essence
few drops green food colouring
40 g/1½ oz pistachio nuts, chopped

Melt the butter until just soft enough to pour. Sift the flour with the salt twice. Place the eggs and sugar in a bowl over a pan of hot water and whisk until thickened. Remove from the heat and whisk until cold. Alternatively use an electric mixer. Carefully fold in half the flour, then the melted butter and lastly the remaining flour. Divide into two portions. Flavour and colour one portion with the almond essence and food colouring.

Place alternate spoonfuls of the mixtures in a lined, greased and floured 30 × 25-cm/12 × 10-inch roasting tin. Sprinkle over the pistachio nuts and bake in a moderate oven for 40–45 minutes, until golden. Cool on a wire tray then cut into squares.

To freeze: Pack in rigid containers in separated layers. Seal and label.
To serve: Unpack and spread out on a serving dish to defrost.
Makes 24

FREEZING HINT

If you have underfloor central heating and wonder whether this will affect your freezer, it will not in fact make any difference to its safe and efficient working.

189 Lemon stars

190 Spritzies

189 Lemon stars

You will need . . .

Cooking time
about 15 minutes

Oven setting
160°C, 325°F, Gas Mark 3

Storage time
6 months

Defrosting time
30 minutes at room temperature

200 g/7 oz plain flour
2 tablespoons cornflour
$\frac{1}{4}$ teaspoon ground cinnamon
175 g/6 oz soft margarine
100 g/4 oz golden syrup
finely grated zest of 2 lemons
For the filling:
75 g/3 oz butter
175 g/6 oz icing sugar
1–2 tablespoons lemon juice

Sift the flour with the cornflour and cinnamon. Beat together the margarine and syrup until light and fluffy. Gradually stir in the dry ingredients and grated lemon zest, until the mixture is smooth.

Place in a piping bag fitted with a star nozzle and press out stars on to greased baking trays. Bake in a moderate oven for about 15 minutes, until pale golden. Cool on a wire tray.

To make the filling, cream the butter and icing sugar and beat in sufficient lemon juice to flavour without over-softening the mixture. Use to sandwich the biscuits together in pairs.

To freeze: Pack carefully in a rigid container in separated layers, or in single layers in polythene bags. Seal and label.
To serve: Unpack while still frozen and spread out on a serving dish. Dust lightly with icing sugar, if liked.
Makes about 20 pairs

FREEZING HINT

Write out labels and stick them on empty polythene bags before filling the bags with food. It is difficult to make a label adhere to a knobbly pack.

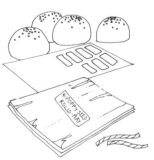

190 Spritzies

You will need . . .

Cooking time
8–10 minutes

Oven setting
190°C, 375°F, Gas Mark 5

Storage time
6 months

Defrosting time
30 minutes at room temperature

225 g/8 oz plain flour
$\frac{1}{4}$ teaspoon salt
175 g/6 oz butter, softened
100 g/4 oz castor sugar
1 egg
1 teaspoon vanilla essence
quartered glacé cherries and chopped angelica for decorating

Sift the flour and salt together. Cream the butter and sugar until light and fluffy. The mixture must be really soft. Beat in the egg and vanilla essence. Fold in the flour and mix until well blended.

Place the dough in a piping bag fitted with a star nozzle and press out 15-cm/6-inch strips of dough on to ungreased baking sheets. Form each strip into a circle and carefully press the edges together without damaging the pattern. Decorate the spritzies with cherry and angelica.

Bake in a moderately hot oven for 8–10 minutes, until pale golden. Cool on a wire tray.

To freeze: Pack in separated layers in a rigid container or in polythene bags. Seal and label.
To serve: Unpack and spread out on a serving dish to defrost.
Makes 20–24

FREEZING HINT

If the freezer site is in a damp atmosphere, polish the cabinet frequently with a silicone polish so beads of moisture cannot accumulate on the outside surface.

191 Almond lace cookies

You will need . . .

75 g/3 oz blanched almonds
75 g/3 oz butter
75 g/3 oz castor sugar
50 g/2 oz plain flour
pinch salt
pinch ground mace

Cooking time
6–8 minutes

Oven setting
200°C, 400°F, Gas Mark 6

Storage time
6 months

Defrosting time
30 minutes at room
temperature

Soak the almonds in boiling water for 5 minutes then drain on kitchen paper and shred finely. Cream the butter and sugar until light and fluffy. Sift together the flour, salt and mace and stir into the creamed mixture with the almonds.

Place walnut-sized pieces of the mixture on non-stick baking trays (or trays lined with non-stick paper) and allow plenty of room for the cookies to spread. Bake in a moderately hot oven for 6–8 minutes, until golden round the edges.

Remove from the oven, lift off the cookies while still hot and curl round a rolling pin. Cool on a wire tray.

To freeze: Pack carefully in a rigid container. Seal and label.
To serve: Unpack and arrange on a serving dish to defrost.
Makes about 15

FREEZING HINT

To avoid sticking to the pan and burning, defrost fruit for stewing over gentle heat and when the juices run increase the heat.

192 Fairy trumpets

You will need . . .

3 egg whites
175 g/6 oz castor sugar
50 g/2 oz plain flour
75 g/3 oz margarine, melted
few drops almond essence

Cooking time
5–6 minutes

Oven setting
200°C, 400°F, Gas Mark 6

Storage time
6 months

Defrosting time
30 minutes at room
temperature

Place the egg whites and sugar in a basin and whisk until smooth only. Sift the flour and add to the mixture with the melted margarine and a little almond essence.

Spread the mixture thinly in squares on greased non-stick baking trays or ones lined with non-stick paper. Bake in a moderately hot oven for 5–6 minutes, until pale golden.

Remove from the oven, lift the cookies off while still hot and curl closely round the end of a cream horn tin or handle of a small wooden spoon. If the cookies harden before you can curl them, return the tray to the oven for a few moments, then try again. Cool on a wire tray.

To freeze: Pack carefully in layers with dividers. Seal and label.
To serve: Unpack and spread out on a serving dish to defrost.
Makes 15–20

FREEZING HINT

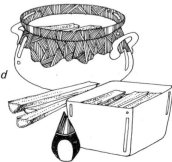

To improve the colour of garden rhubarb for freezing, make up a medium strength sugar syrup, and tint it pink with vegetable food colouring. Use to poach the prepared rhubarb for a few minutes, until just tender. Cool and freeze in the syrup.

193 Pineapple chiffon ring

You will need . . .

Cooking time
35–40 minutes

Oven setting
180°C, 350°F, Gas Mark 4

Storage time
4–6 months

Defrosting time
4 hours at room temperature

225 g/8 oz canned crushed pineapple
   with syrup
about 175 ml/6 fl oz milk
1 egg, separated
175 g/6 oz castor sugar
225 g/8 oz plain flour
½ teaspoon baking powder
½ teaspoon salt
4 tablespoons corn oil
For the filling:
40 g/1½ oz soft margarine
100 g/4 oz icing sugar, sifted

Drain the syrup from the pineapple and make up to 250 ml/
8 fl oz with milk. Whisk the egg white until stiff. Add 50 g/
2 oz sugar and whisk until thick and glossy.

Sift the flour, baking powder and salt into a bowl and
stir in the remaining sugar. Pour in the oil and half the milk
mixture and mix well. Add the egg yolk and remaining
milk mixture and beat for 1 minute. Fold in the egg white
mixture and place in a greased and floured 23-cm/9-inch
ring tin. Bake in a moderate oven for 35–40 minutes. Cool
on a wire tray then split into two layers.

Cream the margarine and icing sugar until smooth.
Reserve a little to pipe a decorative border and beat the
crushed pineapple into the remainder. Sandwich the cake
layers together, pipe a border and dust the top with icing
sugar.

To freeze: Open freeze on a firm base until solid then
cover with a polythene container or bag. Seal and label.
To serve: Uncover and place on a serving dish to defrost.

FREEZING HINT

*Food frozen in roasting bags can
be defrosted and reheated in dry
heat in the oven, or in a pan of
boiling water.*

Ginger
194 ring with lime icing

You will need . . .

Cooking time
1–1¼ hours

Oven setting
150°C, 300°F, Gas Mark 2

Storage time
4–6 months

Defrosting time
4 hours at room temperature

225 g/8 oz plain flour
3 teaspoons ground ginger
½ teaspoon bicarbonate of soda
50 g/2 oz castor sugar
100 g/4 oz black treacle
100 ml/4 fl oz milk
2 eggs, beaten
100 g/4 oz soft margarine
For the icing:
3 tablespoons lime juice cordial
25 g/1 oz butter
150 g/5 oz icing sugar, sifted

Sift the flour with the ginger and bicarbonate of soda
into a bowl. Add all the remaining ingredients for the
cake and beat for 2–3 minutes until well blended.

Spoon into a greased and floured 24-cm/9½-inch ring
tin and bake in a cool oven for 1–1¼ hours, until firm to the
touch. Cool in the tin for 10 minutes then turn out on a wire
rack.

Place the lime juice cordial and butter in a saucepan
and heat gently until the butter has melted. Pour into the
icing sugar and beat until smooth. Add a few drops of food
colouring to tint the icing pale green, if liked. Pour over the
cake and allow to set.

To freeze: Open freeze until solid then pack in a polythene
bag. Seal and label.
To serve: Unpack and place on a serving dish to defrost.

FREEZING HINT

*If cakes are to be stored in the
freezer for more than 2 weeks, it is
better to use buttercream instead
of glacé icing, as the latter tends
to crack when defrosted, especially
if it is rather thick.*

195 Coconut ring cake

You will need . . .

Cooking time
45 minutes

Oven setting
160°C, 325°F, Gas Mark 3

Storage time
4–6 months

Defrosting time
4 hours at room temperature

225 g/8 oz butter
225 g/8 oz castor sugar
4 eggs
225 g/8 oz self-raising flour
6 tablespoons desiccated coconut
For the filling:
100 g/4 oz butter
175 g/6 oz icing sugar, sifted
½ teaspoon vanilla essence

Cream the butter and sugar together until light and fluffy. Beat in the eggs, one at a time, then fold in the flour and 4 tablespoons of the coconut.

Spoon the mixture into a well greased 24-cm/9½-inch spring-form ring tin and smooth the top. Bake in a moderate oven for 45 minutes. Turn out on a wire tray and sprinkle on the remaining coconut while still warm.

To make the filling, cream together the butter and icing sugar and beat in the vanilla essence.

To freeze: Open freeze the cake until solid then pack in a polythene bag. Pack the filling separately in a small polythene container. Seal and label.

To serve: Unpack the cake and place on a serving dish to defrost. Uncover the container of filling. When defrosted, beat the filling until fluffy and pipe into the centre of the ring cake.

FREEZING HINT

A little tea left in the pot is often thrown away, but could be poured into an ice cube tray and the tea cubes saved for refreshing iced tea and lemon drinks. Oddly enough, a tea cube added to beef stew improves the flavour.

196 Cranberry sauce cake

You will need . . .

Cooking time
45–55 minutes

Oven setting
180°C, 350°F, Gas Mark 4

Storage time
4–6 months

Defrosting time
3 hours at room temperature

225 g/8 oz plain flour
1 teaspoon baking powder
1 teaspoon bicarbonate of soda
½ teaspoon salt
½ teaspoon ground cinnamon
½ teaspoon ground nutmeg
100 g/4 oz carrot, grated
100 g/4 oz cranberry sauce
225 g/8 oz soft brown sugar
160 ml/5½ fl oz oil
2 eggs
50 g/2 oz icing sugar, sifted

Sift the flour, baking powder, bicarbonate of soda, salt and spices into a bowl. Add the grated carrot, cranberry sauce, sugar, oil and eggs and beat until well blended.

Pour the mixture into a greased 23-cm/9-inch ring tin and bake in a moderate oven for 45–55 minutes, until well risen and firm to the touch.

Cool in the tin for 10 minutes then turn out on a wire tray. Mix the icing sugar with a little hot water and trickle over the top of the cake. Cool.

To freeze: Open freeze until solid then pack in a polythene bag. Seal and label.

To serve: Unwrap while frozen and place on a serving dish.

FREEZING HINT

When using freezer jam to fill layer cakes, fill when the layers are still frozen so that the jam will not sink into the cake and make stains.

Sweet bread dough
197 Dutch apple bread

You will need . . .

Cooking time
25 minutes

Oven setting
200°C, 400°F, Gas Mark 6

Storage time
2 months

Defrosting time
4 hours at room temperature

250 ml/8 fl oz milk
225 g/8 oz sugar
1 teaspoon salt
225 g/8 oz margarine
4 tablespoons dried yeast
4 eggs
1.25 kg/2½ lb plain flour
For Dutch apple bread:
25 g/1 oz margarine, melted
225 g/8 oz sliced apple
2 tablespoons sugar
½ teaspoon ground cinnamon

To make the basic dough, bring the milk almost to boiling point. Stir in the sugar, salt and margarine; cool the mixture to lukewarm. Warm a large mixing bowl, pour in 250 ml/ 8 fl oz warm water, sprinkle on the yeast and stir until dissolved. Add the milk mixture and stir well. Add the eggs and 675 g/1½ lb of the flour and beat until smooth. Add the remaining flour and mix until the dough leaves the sides of the bowl clean. Turn out on a floured surface and knead for 5 minutes. Return to the bowl and cover with greased polythene. Allow to rise until double in size, turn out and knead again for 1 minute. Divide into four portions.

To make the Dutch apple bread, shape one portion of dough to fit a 20-cm/8-inch square tin and brush with margarine. Cover with the apple slices and sprinkle with the sugar and cinnamon. Bake in a moderately hot oven for 25 minutes. Cool.

To freeze: Pack in a polythene bag. Seal and label.
To serve: Unpack and place on a serving dish to defrost. Decorate with glacé icing as illustrated.

FREEZING HINT

As an alternative to the apple topping, substitute dried apricot or peach halves and finish as above, with glacé icing.

198 Iced cut cherry ring

You will need . . .

Cooking time
25 minutes

Oven setting
200°C, 400°F, Gas Mark 6

Storage time
2 months

Defrosting time
4 hours at room temperature

1 portion sweet bread dough
(see recipe 197)
25 g/1 oz butter, melted
For the filling:
50 g/2 oz glacé cherries, chopped
50 g/2 oz castor sugar
50 g/2 oz sultanas
For the decoration:
3 tablespoons icing sugar, sifted
few drops corn oil

Mix together the cherries, castor sugar and sultanas. Roll out the dough to a rectangle about 30 × 15 cm/12 × 6 inches and brush with melted butter. Sprinkle the cherry mixture over, then roll up from the long side.

Place the roll on a greased baking tray and curl round to form a circle, joining the ends well together. Cut into the roll with scissors at 2.5-cm/1-inch intervals, cutting about two-thirds of the way through the roll. Turn each slice slightly on its side. Cover with a greased polythene bag and allow to rise until double in size. Bake in a moderately hot oven for 10 minutes then cover with foil and bake for a further 15 minutes. Cool.

Mix the icing sugar and oil and add sufficient warm water (about 1 tablespoon) to make a fairly stiff icing. Use to coat the top of the ring and allow to set.

To freeze: Open freeze until solid then pack in a polythene bag or foil. Seal and label.
To serve: Unpack and place on a serving dish to defrost.

FREEZING HINT

If you find plain glacé icing too sweet, mix the icing sugar with strained lemon juice instead of warm water and use to decorate the sweet bread.

199 Pineapple pinwheels

Streusel-filled
200 sweet bread

You will need . . . 1 portion sweet bread dough (see recipe 197)
For the filling:
225 g/8 oz drained canned crushed pineapple
25 g/1 oz butter, melted
100 g/4 oz soft brown sugar
¼ teaspoon ground mace

Cooking time
25–35 minutes

Oven setting
220°C, 425°F, Gas Mark 7

Storage time
2 months

Defrosting time
4 hours at room temperature

First make the filling. Mix together the crushed pineapple, melted butter, soft brown sugar and mace.

Roll out the dough to a rectangle about 40 × 20 cm/ 16 × 8 inches. Spread with the filling and roll up like a Swiss roll, from the long side. Press the long edge to seal and cut the roll into 16 equal slices.

Well grease a 20-cm/8-inch square foil container. Place in the pinwheels, cut sides downwards. Cover with a greased polythene bag and allow to rise until double in size. Bake in a hot oven for 25–35 minutes. Cool.

To freeze: Cover with lid or foil. Seal and label.
To serve: Uncover and leave to stand in the container until defrosted. Separate the pinwheels and arrange on a serving dish.
Makes 16

You will need . . . 1 portion sweet bread dough (see recipe 197)
25 g/1 oz butter, melted
icing sugar
For the filling:
20 g/¾ oz butter
75 g/3 oz soft brown sugar
1 egg yolk
100 g/4 oz ground walnuts or almonds
few drops vanilla essence
½ teaspoon grated lemon zest
4 teaspoons milk

Cooking time
40–45 minutes

Oven setting
200°C, 400°F, Gas Mark 6
180°C, 350°F, Gas Mark 4

Storage time
2 months

Defrosting time
4 hours at room temperature

First make the filling. Cream the butter and sugar together and beat in the egg yolk. Gradually blend in the nuts, vanilla essence, lemon zest and milk.

Roll out the dough to a rectangle 30 × 23 cm/12 × 9 inches. Brush with melted butter then spread with the filling. Cut across into three strips, each 10 cm/4 inches wide. Roll up each strip from the long side and place together in a greased 1-kg/2-lb loaf tin, sealed edges underneath. Brush with butter and cover with a greased polythene bag. Allow to rise until double in size.

Bake in a moderately hot oven for 15 minutes, then reduce to moderate for a further 25–30 minutes, until the loaf sounds hollow when tapped underneath. Cool. Dredge top generously with icing sugar.

To freeze: Pack in a polythene container or bag. Seal and label.
To serve: Unpack on to a serving dish to defrost.

FREEZING HINT

A sweet glaze to run over fruit tarts or top cakes and pastries can be made by warming a pot of apricot jam with a little lemon juice, then straining and thickening it with arrowroot moistened with water. Pack in small containers and freeze. To use, melt just sufficiently to be spreadable.

FREEZING HINT

When heat-sealing packs, try to make the shape similar to that of commercial packs, so they will store flat, one on top of the other.

Golden
201 cornflake clusters

You will need . . .

Storage time
4–6 months

Defrosting time
1 hour at room temperature

75 g/3 oz butter
3 tablespoons golden syrup
grated zest of 1 orange
50 g/2 oz icing sugar
100 g/4 oz cornflakes
50 g/2 oz glacé cherries, chopped
25 g/1 oz candied peel, chopped
50 g/2 oz seedless raisins
25 g/1 oz angelica, chopped

Place the butter, syrup, orange zest and icing sugar in a large saucepan and heat gently, stirring until smooth.

Remove from the heat and stir in the remaining ingredients. Mix well until coated.

Divide the mixture between 15–20 paper bun cases and allow to stand in a cool place until firm.

To freeze: Open freeze until solid then pack in separated layers in rigid-based containers or polythene bags. Seal and label.
To serve: Unpack and spread on a serving dish to defrost.
Makes 15–20

202 Toffee mallow bars

You will need . . .

Storage time
4–6 months

Defrosting time
30 minutes at room temperature

100 g/4 oz creamy toffee
100 g/4 oz soft margarine
100 g/4 oz marshmallows
½ teaspoon almond essence
50 g/2 oz flaked almonds
100 g/4 oz rice krispies

Break up the toffee, or unwrap individual sweets, and place in a saucepan with the margarine, marshmallows and almond essence. Heat gently until the mixture is smooth.

Remove from the heat and stir in the almonds and krispies, coating well with the mixture.

Press into a greased Swiss roll tin and smooth the top lightly with a rolling pin. Cool and cut into 5-cm/2-inch squares.

To freeze: Pack in rigid containers or polythene bags in carefully separated layers. Seal and label.
To serve: Unpack and spread out on a serving dish to defrost.
Makes about 20

FREEZING HINT

Cook fruits which tend to discolour with strongly-coloured fruits — apples with blackberries, pears with cherries — to successfully disguise their tendency to turn brown.

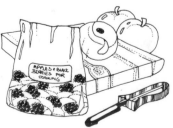

FREEZING HINT

Clean water collected from defrosting your freezer is extremely soft and useful for washing your hair, topping up batteries, filling the steam iron and watering house plants.

Chocolate
203 crunch fingers

204 Hubble-bubbles

You will need . . .
50 g/2 oz butter
4 tablespoons golden syrup
100 g/4 oz plain chocolate, melted
100 g/4 oz cornflakes
50 g/2 oz dried apricots, chopped
50 g/2 oz seedless raisins
50 g/2 oz salted peanuts, chopped

Storage time
4–6 months

Defrosting time
1 hour at room temperature

Melt together the butter and golden syrup and stir in the melted chocolate.

Add the cornflakes, apricots, raisins and peanuts and stir continuously until all are coated with the chocolate mixture.

Press into a greased Swiss roll tin and roll the top lightly with a rolling pin to flatten. Chill and then cut into fingers.

To freeze: Pack in layers, with dividers, in a rigid-based container, or wrap small quantities in cling film. Seal and label.
To serve: Unpack and spread out on a serving dish to defrost.
Makes 15–20

You will need . . .
50 g/2 oz dried apple rings
50 g/2 oz glacé cherries
50 g/2 oz dried figs
50 g/2 oz stoned raisins
50 g/2 oz bran flakes
5 tablespoons clear honey
desiccated coconut for coating

Storage time
4–6 months

Defrosting time
30 minutes at room temperature

Pour boiling water over the apple rings and allow to stand for 5 minutes. Drain and pat dry with kitchen paper. Mince or very finely chop the apple rings, cherries, figs and raisins. Finely crush the bran flakes.

Mix the minced fruit, crushed bran flakes and honey and press the mixture together. Form into small balls, each about the size of a walnut, and roll in coconut. If liked, place each ball in a small paper case.

To freeze: Pack in a rigid container in layers with dividers. Seal and allow to mature at room temperature for 2 days. Label.
To serve: Unpack and arrange on a serving dish to defrost.
Makes about 20

FREEZING HINT

If you find nothing else will write legibly on a freezer pack, and you have no chinagraph pencil or wax crayon, use a lipstick.

FREEZING HINT

When you have time, make sweets and candies to be given as gifts at Christmas and freeze them in foil trays, covered with cling film, until the festive season comes round.

205 Oatmeal crunchies

You will need . . .

Cooking time
10–12 minutes

Oven setting
180°C, 350°F, Gas Mark 4

Storage time
6 months

Defrosting time
30 minutes at room
temperature

75 g/3 oz butter
75 g/3 oz soft brown sugar
100 g/4 oz castor sugar
1 egg
75 g/3 oz plain flour
½ teaspoon salt
½ teaspoon bicarbonate of soda
grated zest of 1 orange
175 g/6 oz rolled oats

Cream the butter and sugars until fluffy. Gradually add the egg. Sift the flour with the salt and bicarbonate of soda and add to the creamed mixture with the orange zest and rolled oats.

Shape into rolls about 5 cm/2 inches in diameter, wrap in foil or cling film and chill.

Cut the dough into slices about 5 mm/¼ inch thick and place the rounds well apart on baking trays. Bake in a moderate oven for 10–12 minutes. Cool.

To freeze: Pack in rigid containers. Seal and label.
To serve: Unpack and spread out on a serving dish to defrost.
Makes about 25

206 Carrot sparkles

You will need . . .

Cooking time
10–12 minutes

Oven setting
190°C, 375°F, Gas Mark 5

Storage time
6 months

Defrosting time
30 minutes at room
temperature

225 g/8 oz soft margarine
100 g/4 oz castor sugar
250 g/9 oz plain flour
½ teaspoon salt
½ teaspoon ground mace
¼ teaspoon ground mixed spice
1 teaspoon vanilla essence
1 egg
175 g/6 oz carrot, finely grated
50 g/2 oz nuts, finely chopped
castor sugar for sprinkling

Cream the margarine and sugar until light and fluffy. Sift the flour with the salt and spices and stir into the creamed mixture with the vanilla essence, egg, carrot and nuts. Mix well.

Place small spoonfuls of the mixture on to greased baking trays and flatten with a palette knife. Bake in a moderately hot oven for 10–12 minutes, until the biscuits are golden round the edges. Sprinkle with castor sugar while still warm. Cool.

To freeze: Pack in a rigid container. Seal and label.
To serve: Unpack and spread out on a serving dish to defrost.
Makes about 36

FREEZING HINT

To make iced lemon tea quickly, take frozen cubes made with double-strength tea and lemon juice (1 tablespoon lemon juice to 600 ml/1 pint double-strength tea). Half-fill heatproof glasses with the cubes and top up with boiling water. Add sugar to taste and stir.

FREEZING HINT

Nuts frozen in the shell take up more space than shelled nuts, but they are easier to crack when defrosted after freezing. It is always worth freezing surplus nuts after Christmas as they are often unobtainable at other times.

Butterscotch
207 flake biscuits

You will need . . .

Cooking time
8–10 minutes

Oven setting
200°C, 400°F, Gas Mark 6

Storage time
6 months

Defrosting time
30 minutes at room
temperature

225 g/8 oz butter
350 g/12 oz soft brown sugar
2 eggs
1 teaspoon vanilla essence
450 g/1 lb self-raising flour
pinch salt
50 g/2 oz white chocolate or frozen
   Mars Bar, grated

Cream the butter and sugar until light and fluffy. Beat in the eggs and vanilla essence. Mix in the flour, salt and grated chocolate to make a firm dough.

Shape into rolls about 5 cm/2 inches in diameter, wrap in foil or cling film and chill.

Slice the dough thinly and place the rounds on baking trays. Bake in a moderately hot oven for 8–10 minutes. Cool.

To freeze: Pack in rigid containers. Seal and label.
To serve: Unpack and spread out on a serving dish to defrost.
Makes 30–40

FREEZING HINT

This type of biscuit dough is excellent to freeze unbaked. Shape into rolls, wrap and freeze. Defrost and slice the rolls while still chilled for best results.

208 Mincemeat stars

You will need . . .

Cooking time
8–10 minutes

Oven setting
200°C, 400°F, Gas Mark 6

Storage time
4–6 months

Defrosting time
30 minutes at room
temperature

225 g/8 oz margarine
100 g/4 oz castor sugar
250 g/9 oz golden syrup
¼ teaspoon almond essence
500 g/1 lb 2 oz plain flour
1 teaspoon baking powder
½ teaspoon salt
about 450 g/1 lb mincemeat
When serving:
icing sugar to sprinkle

Cream the margarine and sugar and gradually beat in the syrup and almond essence. Sift the flour with the baking powder and salt and add to the creamed mixture, mixing to a firm dough.

Shape into rolls about 7.5 cm/3 inches in diameter, wrap in foil or cling film and chill.

Slice the dough thinly and place on baking trays. Drop a little mincemeat into the centre of each round and pinch up the edges to make stars. Bake in a moderately hot oven for 8–10 minutes, until pale golden. Cool.

To freeze: Pack in rigid containers, in layers with dividers. Seal and label.
To serve: Unpack and spread out on a serving dish to defrost. Dust with icing sugar.
Makes about 40

FREEZING HINT

The waxed paper liners in breakfast cereal packs can be smoothed flat, cut into pieces and used as dividers between items such as small cuts of meat, beefburgers and small cakes.

Essential extras

No book for freezer cooks would be complete without a few of those basic extras you will always find room to store. Here is a selection of sauces, both sweet and savoury, and a recipe for the famous uncooked freezer jam, plus a small section devoted entirely to those ever-useful items, pancakes. Suggestions for exciting snacks have not been forgotten. As snacks always seem to be required in a hurry, these, including both fried and toasted sandwiches, come straight from the freezer and take a maximum of 30 minutes to arrive piping hot on the table or tray.

To finish in style, you will find suggestions for four different party menus, showing you how to make use of just a few of the recipes given in this book.

Whisked 210 savoury sauce

209 Newburg sauce

(illustrated on frontispiece)

You will need . . .

Cooking time
about 15 minutes

Storage time
4–6 months

Defrosting time
4 hours at room temperature

50 g/2 oz butter
2 teaspoons Worcestershire sauce
50 g/2 oz flour
300 ml/½ pint milk
300 ml/½ pint single cream
3 egg yolks
3 tablespoons dry sherry

Melt the butter and blend in the Worcestershire sauce. Add the flour and stir until smooth. Gradually stir in the milk and cream and bring to the boil, stirring, until the sauce thickens. Remove from the heat and beat in the egg yolks and sherry. Reheat the sauce but do not boil. Cool.

To freeze: Pack in 300-ml/½-pint quantities in polythene containers. Seal and label.
To serve: Defrost still sealed in the pack, then turn into a saucepan and add 225 g/8 oz cooked fish or shellfish. Reheat to boiling point but do not allow to boil. Season.

Variation: To flavour 300 ml/½ pint basic sauce.
Chicken or Turkey à la king – Melt 25 g/1 oz butter and fry 100 g/4 oz sliced mushrooms until golden. Stir in the sauce, 175 g/6 oz cooked peas and 350 g/12 oz cooked chicken or turkey. Reheat gently to boiling point and cook for 3 minutes. Taste and adjust the seasoning.

FREEZING HINT

To finish a sauce which seems to have lost its gloss after freezing, add a little butter or remove from the heat and whisk in an egg yolk.

You will need . . .

Cooking time
about 10 minutes

Storage time
4–6 months

Defrosting time
4 hours at room temperature

generous 1 litre/2 pints milk
75 g/3 oz butter
75 g/3 oz flour
¼ teaspoon ground nutmeg
salt and ground black pepper

Place the milk, butter and flour in a saucepan and whisk over moderate heat until smooth. Add the nutmeg and a little salt and pepper and bring to the boil, whisking all the time. Cook gently for 2 minutes, stirring. Cool.

To freeze: Pack in 300-ml/½-pint quantities in polythene containers. Seal and label.
To serve: Defrost still sealed in the pack.

Variations: To flavour 300 ml/½ pint basic sauce.
Creamy curry sauce – Fry 1 chopped onion in 25 g/1 o butter. Stir in 1 tablespoon curry powder and fry for minutes, stirring. Add the sauce and a crumbled stock cub and bring to the boil, stirring to blend.
Prawn and olive sauce for fish – Melt 25 g/1 oz butter an sauté 50 g/2 oz sliced button mushrooms until soft. Stir i 2 tablespoons chopped prawns, 2 tablespoons choppe stuffed green olives and 1 teaspoon lemon juice. Add th sauce, bring to the boil, stirring, and adjust seasoning.

FREEZING HINT

The same basic sauce can be used to make parsley sauce by adding 2 tablespoons chopped parsley and extra seasoning; or cheese sauce by adding 1 teaspoon made mustard and 75 g/3 oz grated Cheddar cheese.

211 Italian wine sauce

You will need . . .

Cooking time
about 35 minutes

Storage time
4–6 months

Defrosting
Reheat from frozen in a saucepan

2 tablespoons olive oil
2 medium onions, sliced
1 clove garlic, crushed
100 g/4 oz button mushrooms, sliced
150 ml/¼ pint robust red wine
450 ml/¾ pint beef stock
2 tablespoons tomato purée
1 teaspoon dried oregano
½ teaspoon dried basil
1 (396-g/14-oz) can tomatoes
salt and ground black pepper
1 tablespoon cornflour
12 black olives, stoned

Heat the oil and fry the onion and garlic until soft. Add the mushrooms and cook, stirring, for 3 minutes. Pour in the wine and stock then add the tomato purée, herbs and tomatoes and their liquid. Season to taste and bring to the boil, stirring.

Cook gently for 20 minutes, stirring from time to time. Moisten the cornflour with a little cold water, stir into the sauce and bring to the boil again. Cook for 2 minutes then add the olives. If a thicker sauce is desired, increase the amount of cornflour. Cool.

To freeze: Pack in polythene containers. Seal and label.
To serve: Turn the frozen sauce into a saucepan and bring slowly to boiling point, stirring frequently. Serve with buttered pasta.

FREEZING HINT
To make a more substantial pasta sauce, stir 100 g/4 oz well-drained mussels from a jar into 300 ml/½ pint of the basic sauce and simmer for 5 minutes.

212 Raisin sauce

You will need . . .

Cooking time
about 15 minutes

Storage time
4–6 months

Defrosting time
15 minutes in boiling water from frozen

350 ml/12 fl oz water
50 g/2 oz soft brown sugar
1½ teaspoons dry mustard
1 tablespoon cornflour
3 tablespoons vinegar
50 g/2 oz seedless raisins
15 g/½ oz butter

Place the water, sugar and mustard in a saucepan and stir until smooth.

Moisten the cornflour with the vinegar, add to the pan and bring to the boil, stirring constantly.

Sprinkle in the raisins and cook gently for 10 minutes, until the raisins are plump. Add the butter, stir until melted and cool.

To freeze: Pack in two boiling bags. Seal and label.
To serve: Place the frozen bag of sauce in a pan of boiling water, bring back to the boil and simmer for 15 minutes. Serve with boiled ham or gammon, or with tongue.

FREEZING HINT
This sauce can be defrosted and reheated in the bag, in the pan in which you are boiling the ham or tongue. A small quantity of left-over sauce can be added to the ham stock with vegetables to make a soup.

Lemon
213 butterscotch sauce

Minty
214 marshmallow sauce

You will need . . .

2 tablespoons lemon juice
2 tablespoons water
350 g/12 oz soft brown sugar
225 g/8 oz golden syrup
175 ml/6 fl oz evaporated milk

Cooking time
about 15 minutes

Storage time
4–6 months

Defrosting time
2 hours at room temperature
and reheat in a saucepan if
required

Place the lemon juice, water and sugar in a saucepan and heat gently, stirring, until the sugar dissolves.

Add the golden syrup, stir and bring to the boil. Cook gently without stirring for about 3 minutes, until golden brown and the temperature reaches 115°C/235°F on a sugar thermometer.

Remove from the heat and stir in the evaporated milk until the mixture is smooth. Cool.

To freeze: Pack in small quantities in polythene containers. Seal and label.
To serve: Defrost still sealed in the pack. Serve cold over plain puddings and cakes. If a hot sauce is required, place a tablespoon of water in a small saucepan before adding the defrosted sauce. Heat gently, stirring all the time, and serve over ice cream.

You will need . . .

300 ml/½ pint water
225 g/8 oz castor sugar
225 g/8 oz marshmallows
pinch salt
2 teaspoons cornflour
few drops peppermint essence
few drops green food colouring
(optional)

Cooking time
10–15 minutes

Storage time
4–6 months

Defrosting time
10 minutes in boiling water
from frozen

Place the water and sugar in a saucepan over gentle heat and stir until the sugar dissolves. Bring to the boil and simmer for 5 minutes.

Add the marshmallows and salt and stir until quite smooth. Moisten the cornflour with a tablespoon of water, add to the sauce and bring to the boil, stirring constantly. Simmer for 2 minutes, stirring.

Remove from the heat. Add peppermint essence to taste and a few drops of food colouring, if liked. Cool.

To freeze: Pack in small quantities in boiling bags. Seal and label.
To serve: Place the frozen bag of sauce in a pan of boiling water, bring back to the boil and simmer for 10 minutes. Serve over scoops of chocolate or coffee ice cream.

Variation: To flavour 300 ml/½ pint basic sauce.
Chocolate marshmallow sauce – Omit peppermint essence and green colouring and when the sauce is hot stir in 50 g/2 oz grated plain chocolate until melted.

FREEZING HINT

Cut up a whole pizza and wrap and freeze individually for one-portion servings.

FREEZING HINT

To heat sauces from frozen quickly, hold the sealed pack under running water for a couple of minutes or until you can turn the contents out into a saucepan. Place over low heat, stirring occasionally until heated through.

215 Brandy berry sauce

Orange and 216 raspberry freezer jam

You will need . . .

225 g/8 oz fresh cranberries
150 ml/¼ pint pineapple juice
175 g/6 oz sugar
1 teaspoon grated orange zest
½ teaspoon grated lemon zest
3 tablespoons brandy
25 g/1 oz butter
pinch salt

Cooking time
12–15 minutes

Storage time
4–6 months

Defrosting time
15 minutes in boiling water
from frozen

Pick over the cranberries and place them in a saucepan with the pineapple juice, sugar and fruit zests.

Bring to the boil and cook gently for about 10 minutes, until the cranberries have all burst.

Remove from the heat and stir in the brandy, butter and salt. Cool.

To freeze: Pack in small quantities in boiling bags. Seal and label.

To serve: Place the frozen bag of sauce in a pan of boiling water, bring back to the boil and simmer for 15 minutes. Serve over scoops of vanilla ice cream.

You will need . . .

1 kg/2¼ lb raspberries
1.5 kg/3½ lb castor sugar
1 orange
3 tablespoons lemon juice
1 orange jelly
250 ml/8 fl oz commercial fruit pectin

Storage time
12 months

Defrosting time
30 minutes at room
temperature

Place the raspberries and castor sugar in a bowl and allow to stand for 1 hour. As the juice begins to run from the fruit, stir, and stir again at intervals until the sugar is fully dissolved. This will take several hours.

Meanwhile, finely grate the zest from the orange and squeeze the juice. Place the orange juice, zest, lemon juice and orange jelly in a saucepan and heat gently until the jelly dissolves.

Pour the jelly liquid into the fruit mixture with the pectin and stir well until the jam begins to thicken.

To freeze: Pack in small polythene or freezer-tested glass containers. Seal and label.
To serve: Defrost still sealed in the pack.
Note: Fruit pectin can be bought at a good general chemist.

FREEZING HINT

Sauces frozen in boiling bags can be turned out with little waste if one corner is snipped off the bag and the sauce pressed out into a serving jug.

FREEZING HINT

Freezer jams made with soft berry fruit, sugar, lemon juice and liquid fruit pectin have a fresh taste which is hard to beat. Storage time is a whole year and, as no cooking is required, none of the precious fruit is boiled away.

You will need . . .

225 g/8 oz plain flour
pinch salt
3 eggs
2 tablespoons oil
600 ml/1 pint milk
oil for frying

Cooking time
about 20 minutes

Oven setting
190°C, 375°F, Gas Mark 5

Storage time
4–6 months

Defrosting time
4 hours at room temperature

Sift the flour and salt into a bowl and make a deep well in the centre. Drop in the eggs, oil and milk and whisk steadily until the mixture forms a smooth thin batter. Allow the batter to stand for about 30 minutes if possible, then beat again before using.

Heat a little oil in an omelette pan or small frying pan. Pour about 2–3 tablespoons of the batter into the centre of the pan, tilting it to allow the batter to coat the base evenly. Cook until golden brown underneath then toss over and cook the other side.

Slide on to a plate and cool while the next is cooking. Add a little more oil to the pan each time. Pile up the cooled pancakes with dividers.

To freeze: Pack the stacked pancakes in foil or a polythene bag. Seal and label.
To serve: Defrost still sealed in the pack.
Makes 15–20

You will need . . .

75 g/3 oz plain flour
25 g/1 oz cornflour
generous pinch salt
1 egg
175 ml/6 fl oz water
oil for frying
For the filling:
50 g/2 oz shelled prawns, chopped
2 tablespoons chopped spring onion
75 g/3 oz beansprouts
1 teaspoon soy sauce

Cooking time
about 20 minutes

Storage time
2–3 months

Defrosting time
12–15 minutes in hot oil from frozen

Sift the flour, cornflour and salt. Add the egg and water and beat with a wooden spoon, gradually drawing in the dry ingredients, to make a smooth thin batter.

Mix together all the ingredients for the filling.

Reserve 2 tablespoons of the batter and use the remainder to make 8 large very thin pancakes, but cook on one side only until the uncooked surface looks dry. Pile up the filling in the centre of the cooked sides. Fold two sides of each pancake in over the filling, brush the folded edges with the reserved batter, then roll up neatly from an open end and press gently to seal.

To freeze: Wrap individually in foil or cling film, then pack together in a polythene container or bag. Seal and label.
To serve: Unwrap and fry from frozen in deep hot oil for 12–15 minutes until brown and crisp. Serve hot, garnished with mustard and cress.
Serves 4

FREEZING HINT

Plain pancakes are marvellous freezables. Pack them when cold, with concertina dividers. Reheat from the frozen state in an omelette pan just smeared with butter or oil.

FREEZING HINT

Vegetarians will enjoy stuffed pancake rolls filled with sprouting vegetables and nuts. Always keep a supply of basic pancakes in the freezer, ready for filling.

Spinach
219 pancake gratin

You will need . . .

Cooking time
about 15 minutes

Oven setting
220°C, 425°F, Gas Mark 7

Storage time
4–6 months

Defrosting time
30 minutes in the oven from frozen

225 g/8 oz frozen chopped spinach
300 ml/½ pint whisked savoury sauce
  (see recipe 210)
1 teaspoon French mustard
salt and ground black pepper
½ teaspoon ground nutmeg
100 g/4 oz Cheddar cheese, grated
8 basic pancakes (see recipe 217)
1 tablespoon flaked almonds

Place the frozen spinach in a saucepan and defrost over gentle heat, stirring frequently. Continue to cook, stirring from time to time, until all excess moisture has evaporated.

Gradually add the sauce to combine well with the spinach, then add the mustard and other seasonings. When the mixture is hot but not boiling, sprinkle in most of the grated cheese, stir and remove from the heat.

Divide the filling among the pancakes, roll them up and arrange side by side in a greased shallow foil container. Sprinkle the remaining cheese and flaked almonds over the pancake rolls and cool.

To freeze: Cover with foil. Seal and label.
To serve: Loosen foil cover and reheat in a hot oven for 20 minutes. Remove cover and return to the oven for a further 10 minutes, to brown the top. Serve hot, garnished with mustard and cress and a tomato slice.
Serves 4

FREEZING HINT

Spinach does not necessarily need blanching, but cook it completely, drain well and chop or purée before freezing. It will then pack into a fraction of the space required by uncooked spinach.

220 Mandarin crêpes

You will need . . .

Cooking time
about 25 minutes

Oven setting
220°C, 425°F, Gas Mark 7

Storage time
4–6 months

Defrosting time
25 minutes in the oven from frozen

2 tablespoons milk
1 tablespoon brandy
450 ml/¾ pint basic whisked pancake
  batter (see recipe 217)
oil for frying
For the filling:
1 (312-g/11-oz) can mandarin oranges
4 tablespoons orange jelly marmalade
1 teaspoon arrowroot

Add the milk and brandy to the basic pancake batter and beat well. Use to make 8 large very thin pancakes.

Place the mandarin oranges and their syrup in a saucepan with the marmalade. Stir well and heat gently until the marmalade has melted. Using a slotted draining spoon, remove the mandarin segments from the sauce and divide among the pancakes. Fold the pancakes lightly into four, with the filling inside, and arrange in a greased shallow foil container.

Moisten the arrowroot with a tablespoon of water, add to the marmalade mixture and bring to the boil, stirring. As soon as the mixture clears and thickens slightly pour over the folded pancakes. Cool.

To freeze: Cover with lid or foil. Seal and label.
To serve: Uncover and reheat from frozen in a hot oven for 25 minutes.
Serves 4

FREEZING HINT

Pancakes are easy to freeze in made-up dishes, either stuffed and rolled, layered with fillings, or folded. If covered with sauce, reheat foil containers uncovered. If no sauce, cover with foil while reheating and remove cover for the last 5 minutes.

221 Skillet sandwiches

You will need . . .

Storage time
1 month

Defrosting time
4–6 minutes in hot oil from frozen

175 g/6 oz black olives, stoned
3 tablespoons tomato ketchup
3 tablespoons mayonnaise
½ teaspoon Worcestershire sauce
1 tablespoon chopped spring onion
175 g/6 oz Cheddar cheese, grated
8 slices white bread
2 medium tomatoes
When serving:
oil for frying

Chop the olives roughly and place in a basin with the ketchup, mayonnaise and Worcestershire sauce. Add the spring onion and gradually mix in the cheese until well combined.

Trim the bread slices and cut the tomatoes into very thin slices. Spread half the cheesy filling over 4 slices of bread, top with tomato slices and cover with the rest of the filling.

Place the remaining bread slices on top and press lightly. Cut each sandwich into four triangles.

To freeze: Pack in a polythene container or bag, in layers with dividers. Seal and label.
To serve: Unpack while still frozen and shallow fry in hot oil for 2–3 minutes on each side, until golden brown and heated through.
Serves 4

222 Ranch-house toasties

You will need . . .

Storage time
1 month

Defrosting time
6–8 minutes under a hot grill from frozen

1 (425-g/15-oz) can baked beans
1 teaspoon grated onion
100 g/4 oz salami, chopped
2 tablespoons sweet brown pickles
2 tablespoons French mustard
8 slices white bread
butter for spreading
When serving:
few stuffed olives

Mix together the baked beans, onion, salami, pickles and mustard.

Trim the bread slices and spread thinly with butter.

Divide the filling among 4 slices of bread and top with the remaining slices. Press lightly and cut into quarters.

To freeze: Pack in a polythene container or bag, in layers with dividers. Seal and label.
To serve: Unpack while still frozen and toast under a hot grill for 3–4 minutes on each side until well browned and heated through. Serve with stuffed olives, speared on to a cocktail stick.
Serves 4

FREEZING HINT

Make up a batch of sandwiches with different fillings and freeze mixed packs for lunch boxes and picnic baskets.

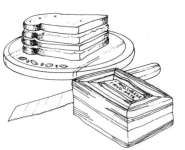

FREEZING HINT

Welsh rarebit mixture can be prepared in quantity, spread on a number of slices of toast, and the resulting rarebits open frozen before packing. The frozen slices arranged on a grid defrost, reheat and brown on top in about 10 minutes under the grill.

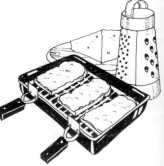

223 Piped potato nests

You will need . . .

Cooking time
about 15 minutes

Oven setting
220°C, 425°F, Gas Mark 7

Storage time
3–4 months

Defrosting time
15–20 minutes in the oven
from frozen

1.75 kg/4 lb potatoes
100 g/4 oz butter
2 eggs
salt and pepper
1 (425-g/15-oz) can minced soya
protein in gravy
When serving:
little beaten egg

Slice the potatoes and cook in lightly salted water until tender. Drain well and mash with the butter, eggs and seasoning to taste.

Put the potato mixture into a piping bag fitted with a star nozzle. Pipe out six 10-cm/4-inch flat circles on baking trays lined with non-stick paper, then pipe one ring on the edge of each to make them into nests.

Divide the soya mince among the nests. Cool.

To freeze: Open freeze until solid then pack in a polythene container, in layers using the non-stick paper as dividers. Seal and label.
To serve: Unpack while still frozen and place on baking sheets, still keeping the non-stick paper underneath. Brush with beaten egg and bake from frozen in a hot oven for 15–20 minutes.
Serves 6

FREEZING HINT

To economise on oven space and fuel, place different foods enclosed in foil parcels on a baking sheet and defrost and cook or defrost and reheat together in the oven.

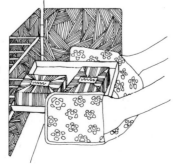

224 Yorkies

You will need . . .

Cooking time
20–25 minutes

Oven setting
200°C, 400°F, Gas Mark 6

Storage time
3–4 months

Defrosting time
15 minutes in the oven from
frozen

100 g/4 oz self-raising flour
pinch salt
2 eggs
300 ml/½ pint milk
½ teaspoon dried mixed herbs
25 g/1 oz dripping or lard
2 faggots or 100 g/4 oz black pudding

Make a batter with the flour, salt, eggs and milk and beat well. Stir in the mixed herbs.

Fit 12 foil tartlet cases into deep bun tins and use the dripping or lard to grease them well. Place in a moderately hot oven for 4 minutes to heat the fat.

Meanwhile, roughly chop the faggots or black pudding. Divide the batter between the foil cases, filling each one about two-thirds full. Place a little faggot or black pudding in the centre of each and bake in the oven for 15–20 minutes, until well risen and pale golden. Cool.

To freeze: Chill the yorkies until firm then pack in their foil cases in a polythene container. Seal and label.
To serve: Unpack and arrange the yorkies, still in their foil cases, on a baking tray. Reheat from frozen in a moderately hot oven for 15 minutes, until crisp.
Serves 6

FREEZING HINT

Mint jelly is tiresome to make, but mint sauce is made in a moment with cubes of frozen chopped mint, a little vinegar and sugar, and sufficient boiling water to dissolve the cube.

225 Drink 'n' dip party

Menu

Curried avocado dip
Herbed cheese dip
carrot curls, celery sticks, tomato quarters, olives
*Creamy chicken liver pâté
small cocktail biscuits and pretzels

Curried avocado dip: Combine the mashed pulp from 2 large ripe avocados with 225 g/8 oz cream cheese and 1 tablespoon curry paste. Gradually beat in a few drops of lemon juice. Fold in 2 tablespoons finely chopped spring onion and season to taste with salt and pepper. Serve piled in a bowl in the centre of a platter, surrounded with potato crisps of various flavours or other dippers.

Herbed cheese dip: Cut the top third off a baby Edam cheese and scoop out the centre with the aid of a grapefruit knife. Cut part of the cheese into large matchsticks and grate the remainder. Mix the grated cheese with 150 ml/¼ pint soured cream and 1 heaped tablespoon finely chopped mixed fresh herbs, and season to taste with French mustard, salt and pepper. Vandyke the edge of the cheese shell with scissors and fill with the herby mixture. Place the filled Edam on a board and serve with carrot curls, celery sticks, tomato quarters, olives and the cheese sticks to use as dippers.

* Recipe from this book.

226 Teatime buffet party

Menu

Grape and cherry fruit salad
*Fairy trumpets
*Coffee and hazelnut roulade
*Pineapple prune freeze
Summer cup

Grape and cherry fruit salad: Slowly dissolve 175 g/6 oz granulated sugar in 2 tablespoons lemon juice made up to 300 ml/½ pint with water. Boil for 2 minutes then set aside to cool. Halve and pip 225 g/8 oz each of black and white grapes. Stone 225 g/8 oz red cherries. Unless the cherries are very sweet and juicy include a few Maraschino cherries as well as the fresh ones. Mix these with the grapes, add 3 peeled and sliced bananas and pour over the lemon syrup. Just before serving, add 2 tablespoons cherry brandy and serve with Fairy trumpets.

Summer cup: Pour 150 ml/¼ pint brandy into a punch bowl. Put a few strawberries and slices of fresh peach in the brandy and allow to stand for at least 1 hour. Pour in 1 litre/1¾ pints rosé wine and 2 large bottles fizzy lemonade. Float several lemon and cucumber slices on the surface and borage flowers if obtainable. Serve in punch cups over crushed ice.

* Recipes from this book.

FREEZING HINT

When planning a special meal for a party, freeze all supplies and pack together in one freezer basket, or on one shelf, clearly marked, to avoid a last-minute hunt for the pâté or parsley butter.

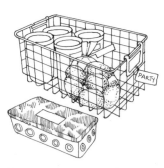

FREEZING HINT

When coconuts are in season freeze some of the flesh grated and moistened with the milk from the coconut. It makes a perfect side dish for curry or adds an exotic touch to fruit salad.

227 Evening buffet party

Menu

*Sparkling beetroot soup
Garlic bread
*Cheese bread
Stuffed egg platter
Sausage spikes

Garlic bread: Slice a small French loaf almost through to the base diagonally at 2-cm/¾-inch intervals. Crush 1 clove of garlic and beat into 75 g/3 oz softened butter, adding extra salt if required. Spread the flavoured butter on each side of the slices and reshape the loaf. Wrap closely in foil and freeze until required. Place the frozen loaf, still wrapped, in a hot oven for about 20 minutes.

Canasta corned eggs: Hard-boil 12 eggs, shell and cut in half lengthways. Scoop out the yolks with a teaspoon and mash with 2 tablespoons mayonnaise and 2 tablespoons very finely chopped piccalilli. Fold in 4 tablespoons drained sweetcorn and season to taste with salt and pepper. Pile up the filling in the egg halves and arrange on a bed of shredded lettuce. Stamp out heart, diamond, spade and club shapes with fancy bridge cutters from thin slices of white bread and fry golden brown in hot oil. Use to garnish the egg halves and scatter with mustard and cress.

Sausage spikes: Use wooden cocktail sticks to spike cooked cocktail sausages with silverskin onions and Maraschino cherries.

* Recipes from this book.

FREEZING HINT

Cheese bread is made in the same way as garlic bread but the cut surfaces are spread with a mixture of softened butter, grated cheese and mustard.

228 Cocktail party

Menu

*Walnut cheese ball
carrot curls, celery sticks, olives, radish roses, pretzels, Melba toast
*Prawns with curried mayonnaise
Savoury tartlets
*Puff cheese whirls

Savoury tartlets: Thinly roll out 450 g/1 lb shortcrust pastry and use to line 24 greased shallow bun tins. Prick well and bake 'blind' in a moderately hot oven for 15–20 minutes, until pale golden. Cool. Fill 12 tartlets with chicken and mushroom filling and 12 with crab and cucumber filling.

Chicken and mushroom filling: Melt 25 g/1 oz butter and use to fry 100 g/4 oz thinly sliced button mushrooms until golden. Reserve 12 slices for garnish then stir in 300 ml/½ pint hot whisked savoury sauce (see recipe 210), 1 egg yolk and 100 g/4 oz chopped cooked chicken. Season to taste, fill the tartlet cases and serve warm, garnished with radish slices and mustard and cress.

Crab and cucumber filling: Combine 100 g/4 oz fresh or canned crab meat, 100 g/4 oz peeled and diced cucumber, 1 tablespoon mayonnaise and 300 ml/½ pint whisked savoury sauce (see recipe 210). Season to taste, garnish the filled tartlets with mustard and cress and tomato fans and serve cold.

* Recipes from this book.

FREEZING HINT

Frozen canapés defrost well, except for the toasted bread used as a base. To keep them crisp after freezing, use thinly cut fried bread instead of toast as a base.

Index